REVIVAL SIGNS

REVIVAL SIGNS

Join the New Spiritual Awakening

Tom Phillips

VISION™
HOUSE
PUBLISHING, INC.
Gresham, Oregon 97030

REVIVAL SIGNS: THE COMING SPIRITUAL AWAKENING
© 1995 by Tom Phillips

Published by Vision House Publishing, Inc.
1217 NE Burnside, Suite 403
Gresham, Oregon 97030

Printed in the United States of America.

International Standard Book Number: 1-885305-15-X

95 96 97 98 99 00 01 02 03 04 - 10 9 8 7 6 5 4 3 2 1

Dedication

To Ouida, my partner in the greatest life a man could have. Thanks, Honey, for the consistent encouragement to write this book and for the support during it.

Thanks

To write a book encouraging others to seek personal and national spiritual awakening is to learn the meaning of humility. The more I wrote about God's awesome power, the more I realized how inadequate I am on my own. And so it was a blessing to work with Mark Cutshall. If this book is useful, clear and vivid, it is because of Mark's tremendous literary gift. I'm so grateful for his help and for his friendship.

Dr. Lewis Drummond, the Billy Graham Professor of Evangelism at Beeson Divinity School and President Emeritus of Southeastern Seminary, has been my spiritual mentor in the area of the Pietistic Movement, spiritual awakening, and evangelism. I'm thankful to Dr. Drummond for being the vessel that God has used to touch my life deeply regarding His plans for our world and for the future.

Dr. Charles Riggs, the Director Emeritus of Counseling and Follow-Up for the Billy Graham Evangelistic Association, has been my spiritual Paul for twenty years. His challenge to my life relative to the Word of God and my walk in the Holy Spirit has exhorted and encouraged me to rest in the Lord for all that He could and would do through me. Also, thanks to Gene Warr and Jack Humphreys for being Barnabases in my spiritual life.

Kathy Maas, the Production and Communications Team Leader for International Students, Inc., has been a vital player in reviewing the manuscript, offering concise suggestions and correction, and personal encouragement.

My thanks also to those who have encouraged this work and reviewed the manuscript where necessary: Wanda Bailey, Dr. Joe Aldrich, Dr. Bob Coleman, Dr. Tim Beougher, Carol Speirs, and the one who has been a major influence in all that God has done to prepare the Church for this great movement of His Spirit that is just beginning—Dr. Billy Graham.

Table of Contents

Introduction: Revival, One Person at a Time   27

1. Ordinary People Living Quiet,
   Anonymous Lives–Until...   37
2. What Is Happening to Our World?   51
3. A Truth We Almost Forgot   73
4. When Broken, Humbled People
   Come Together   103
5. Why Prayer Is the Key   129
6. Unseen Obstacles Ahead   173
7. What Will the New Awakening
   Look Like?   201
8. The Most Important Decision of All   227

Epilogue: Preparing for Personal Revival   249

Appendix: Resource Guide   259

Foreword

Is America in the early stages of a spiritual revival which will overshadow anything we have ever seen before in our nation's history?

Tom Phillips makes a convincing case that this could be true, as he examines some of the significant new ways God is at work touching lives today. Only history will be able to tell us if his thesis is accurate, for we are too near to these events to judge—but no one can read this book and not be touched by the way God is working today in the lives of countless men and women who formerly gave little thought to Christ.

For many years Tom Phillips was a valued member of our team, and I know of few individuals who have a deeper commitment to evangelism and a broader understanding of what is happening spiritually across our land. His book is a vivid and compelling testimony to the truth that the Gospel in all of its fullness is still (in Paul's words) "the power of God for the salvation of everyone who believes." As he recounts, Tom has experienced that truth in his own life, and I believe every reader of his book will experience it too, as they open their hearts to the molding and life-changing power of Jesus Christ.

Billy Graham
Minneapolis, Minnesota
April, 1995

Preface

I was hunched over my desk, writing a report about faith and culture, when my assistant shattered the reflective atmosphere with the intercom buzzer. My long-time friend Tom Phillips, then of the Billy Graham Evangelistic Association, was calling.

After the usual introductory banter about families and current activities, Tom abruptly changed gears, as one does when there is something terribly significant on one's mind but unsure about how to ease into the subject. "George, based on all the information you have about our society today, are we in or about to enter into a time of revival?"

It was a reasonable question, but it made me uneasy. My discomfort was not because I don't want revival—what lover of Christ doesn't yearn to see people transformed to be devoted followers of the Master? I shifted uneasily in my chair not because I didn't have an opinion on the matter—after all, the whole question of shifts in religious beliefs and fervor is something I spend my life evaluating. No, the discomfort was because there is no research technique known to humankind that can effectively predict spiritual revival. When we strive to determine when revival will sweep a nation, we are applying natural means to the assessment of a supernatural phenomenon. I hate to tell people there is no evidence of revival, even if there is none at hand. Somehow, I feel as if I'm betraying the cause of Christ. And instinctively I knew that God could be working in ways that do not get measured by a few questions on a survey. And yet, as a social scientist, I could not allow my emotional ties to Christ and His church to bias my response to provide an optimistic and rosy, if insupportable, portrait of the current spiritual landscape.

So I did what every self-respecting social scientist does: reframe the question around the facts and figures available. I explained that I think we can determine when conditions are unusually ripe for revival and what steps a nation's spiritual leaders might take to prepare for such a return to God. The bottom line was—and is—this: There is a significant spiritual quest taking place in America today that represents an environment in which revival is an extraordinary possibility and a deep need within America.

But I pressed Tom a bit further and noted that our churches are not adequately prepared to sustain a major move of the Holy Spirit. History suggests that when revival has happened, it was preceded by a widespread desire and preparation among church leaders for such revivals. Today, our church leaders are preoccupied with institutional survival and other comparatively trivial issues. If God needs the organized church as an instrument in the transforming of a nation, then America is far from the precipice of revival, I opined. It is one thing to desire mass decisions for Christ; it is another matter to see those expressions of interest nurtured into true conversions through serious discipleship.

Jump forward a year or so. A manuscript arrives at the same desk where I took the phone call alluded to above. It is Tom Phillips' first major written work, a body of thought that has been a lifetime in the making, on the subject that consumes his heart: revival in America. In this thoughtful and valuable book, Tom addresses the issues that have troubled those among us who have prayed for, searched for and struggled to understand revival. I am so grateful to Tom for the many instructive and encouraging perspectives he provides in this book. As every great work does, *Revival Signs* challenges us to reconsider some of our assumptions.

- America has experienced at least three major revivals in the past. However, the next revival need not be limited by the contours of those of the past: God is powerful and creative enough to develop new dimensions beyond anything we might be expecting. Is it feasible that we could be in the midst of a revival and not even realize it because we are looking for something different than what God has ordained? (Reminds me of the frog in the kettle dilemma . . .)

- Ministry in America often becomes a professional activity rather than a God-driven spiritual effort. We run the risk of trying to professionalize revival. But revival is not primarily about better outreach techniques, more efficient management practices or achieving a more precise understanding of God's approach to human transformation. It is about God changing open hearts and about his servants being obedient to their calling. Is it possible that our lust for definable steps to revival or the orderly implementation of tested tactics may retard rather than facilitate spiritual change?

- What a tremendously strategic time this is for revival to happen in America. The cultural diversity within America that has so befuddled policy makers and church leaders has provided God with a chance to influence hundreds and hundreds of cultures around the world by invading those cultures as they converge upon the United States. Are American Christians guilty of pigeon-holing revival as a massive and well-documented shift in the church activity of white adults?

I profited by reading Tom's book. Thankfully, he moves beyond the politically correct notion of enabling do-gooders to "feel your pain" to the spiritually correct notion of letting God, through the Holy Spirit, "heal your pain." With wisdom and humility, Tom raises the possibility that the fourth revival in America may be different from those that preceded it. Indeed, from both a sociological and theological vantage point, why not? Sociologically, everything else taking place in the U.S. today, from politics to consumerism, from education to family dynamics, from commerce to personal relationships, is vastly different than it was just a few years ago—and constantly changing. Theologically, we serve a God whose truths are eternal but whose means are practical. Why shouldn't we expect the God who creates and uses changes to work through a similarly unique process as He renews our hearts and minds these days?

Revival Signs is a work of the heart, a product of one man's lifelong passion to be an agent of spiritual reconciliation of humans with God. In the decade we have worked together, I know of no person who would be more appropriate for the task of discussing the matter of revival. From his days as a pastor to his work as part of the Billy Graham inner circle to his current adventures as the leader of the revitalized International Students ministry, Tom has poured his life into making revival happen. He brings a well-honed set of experiences to this task of discussing God's transforming work within a nation that is spiritually lost but desperately searching. Tom is more than just a godly man writing about his ministry passion; he is a faithful servant compelled by God to share truths about revival. It is a special work by a special man, for a special time and a holy purpose.

I pray that you will give Tom a few hours of your time to dig deeper into the matter of revival, and through the experience allow God to confront your assumptions about how He works.

George Barna
Glendale, California
April, 1995

Notes from Others

World revival is not only possible, but I believe it is probable. Yet it is not automatic. Tom Phillips has done an incredible job in clearly showing the need and the way to genuine revival. I commend this book and pray a wide distribution.

Adrian Rogers
Pastor
Bellevue Baptist Church
Memphis, Tennessee

Only God knows what awaits an unrepentant America. I'm hopeful we will never find out! My friend Tom Phillips describes an emerging spiritual reawakening that is transforming the lives of everyday Americans, and how your life too can be changed forever.

Luis Palau
Portland, Oregon

This book will bring you to your knees and raise your sights to a glorious and thrilling reality—God is on the move! Tom Phillips convincingly points to the mercy drops of revival, compelling the reader to plead for the showers—and heaven knows we need it! The indications are fascinating: a slumbering church is beginning to stir. Tom Phillips chronicles a profound movement that has begun and could touch the soul of a nation.

Ravi Zacharias
Norcross, Georgia

We are on the verge of what may be the greatest spiritual awakening in history. Tom Phillips' insights will help us prepare for it, recognize it, and be a part of it, for God's glory.

Bill Bright
Campus Crusade for Christ Int'l
Orlando, Florida

There has never been a time in the history of the church when God's people have not had a heart-cry for revival. Even in the midst of appalling moral darkness and spiritual declension there has been a heart-cry that God would "tear the heavens open and come down" (Isa. 64:1, The Jerusalem Bible). Speaking for our time, however, I see no hope for the church or for our land outside of a mighty spiritual awakening. What is encouraging is that this longing for revival is being manifested by a deep concern for prayer all across our country and a new emphasis on the need for repentance, brokenness and holiness.

My good friend Tom Phillips has expressed this burden in his timely book, *Revival Signs*. I warmly commend the reading of these chapters concerning the key indicators of the new reawakening that are taking place simultaneously in different parts of the United States of America. Let us join him and multitudes of concerned Christian leaders for a mighty outpouring of the Spirit in true biblical revival.

Stephen F. Olford
Founder and Senior Lecturer
Stephen Olford Center for
Biblical Preaching
Memphis, Tennessee

We all seek revival and renewal, but we may not see what God is doing right before our eyes. Tom Phillips helps us recognize God's working in our nation today. This is a significant book to awaken us to cooperate with God in *His* work.

Jerry E. White
President, The Navigators
Colorado Springs, Colorado

Signs of a coming revival seem to be appearing all around us. Tom Phillips shares some extraordinary insights and encouragement in this "cutting edge" book. Every Christian will be both blessed and challenged by reading it and responding to its message.

Paul A. Cedar
President
Evangelical Free Churches
of America

For you who sense a growing hunger for God in your life, you'll be encouraged by the abundant evidence that we stand on the threshold of a great spiritual awakening. God is up to something! Tom Phillips' extensive study of past awakenings coupled with his present-day widespread exposure to God's workings provides a needed, powerful, practical, yet personal clarification of revival and stirs the soul with hope and anticipation. You'll find helpful guidance and motivation to move from spectator to participant.

Terry Dirks
Vice President, International
Renewal Ministries
Portland, Oregon

Tom Phillips has the heart of the New Testament Philip, an evangelist. To read *Revival Signs* is to catch their hearts.

Jim Gwinn
CRISTA Ministries
Seattle, Washington

A critical need exists for a word of encouragement in today's church. Tom Phillips' book *Revival Signs* meets this need. God is moving in new and fresh ways today. This book will help you get in on it.

Roy J. Fish
Professor of Evangelism
Southwestern Baptist Theological
Seminary
Fort Worth, Texas

At a time when all the tabloids, talk-shows, and ene- mies in high places are slandering our Lord and the Gospel, God has been working quietly to undermine their strategies and revive His work. At this very moment there is a mighty move of God mushrooming to unprecedented levels eclipsing everything to the contrary. A spirit of anticipation is everywhere.

Danny de Leon
Pastor, Templo Calvario Church
Santa Ana, California

Today in America we see two countervailing trends. The one leads to the moral abyss of drugs, immorality, violence and death. The second leads to hope, renewal, caring and life. Clearly God is at work among a needy people bringing men and women into a vital relationship with His Son. The author Tom Phillips (president of International Students and no relation to me) gives docu- mented evidence on the reason for this in *Revival Signs: The Coming Spiritual Awakening*.

Tom Phillips
Former CEO, Raytheon Company
Lexington, Massachusetts

Here is a much-needed book setting forth a much- needed truth. America needs a genuine spiritual awaken- ing. Dr. Phillips' book tells us what that is and the Christian's responsibility to see it occur. I highly recommend the reading, assimilation, and practice of the principles of this excellent volume.

Lewis A. Drummond
Billy Graham Professor of
    Evangelism and
        Church Growth
Beeson Divinity School,
    Samford University
Birmingham, Alabama

After praying for forty-six years for the kind of renewal described in this book, I too am just now feeling that God has begun to birth it in our country. I believe this book accurately describes the historically proven steps of cleansing, transforming, and empowering that have accompanied every God-initiated outpouring of His Spirit. This book is *must* reading, for every Christian searching for answers to our country's moral plunge.

Evelyn Christenson
St. Paul, Minnesota

In what I consider to be darkening days, Tom gives hope showing that God is on the move and we can be part of that. I highly commend *Revival Signs: The Coming Spiritual Awakening*.

Lorne Sanny
Chairman of the Board
    of Directors
The Navigators
Colorado Springs, Colorado

All of us in our Christian walk long for words of encouragement. Here's a book that does just that! This is not a "Pollyanna" treatment, but a significant look at the hopeful signs all around us of spiritual renewal and revival.

Ted. W. Engstrom
President Emeritus
World Vision
Monrovia, California

Revival, One Person at a Time

God is intent on bringing His people to Himself. At certain moments in history, even when many turn away from God, God continues to turn the hearts of men and women to Himself.

Are you open to this likelihood for your church? Your community? This nation? Are you open to the chance that God's Spirit, without warning, could sweep through your own life? I dearly hope so. That's why I wrote this book, to encourage and nurture such a hope.

It's a hope I've cherished for a long time. The seed of it was planted when I was a small child, on a country drive near Corinth, Mississippi, where I grew up. I can still see the tiny shacks from the car window and hear myself asking my mother, "Why do the black people live there, Mom?"

"That's just the way it is, son."

Now fast forward to a small church service near the town of Water Valley, Mississippi, where I was about to give my sermon to my first congregation—all white. In the years since that country ride with my mother, my increasing understanding of God's glorious, planned variety of color in people, and of His wish for our unequivocal acceptance of each other, had grown. I sensed then, as I now am certain, that if an earth-shaking, national awakening is real, then the refreshing winds of the Spirit will touch not just the people in the church pews, but also the most remote, insensitive hearts and the many shades of prejudice and hate that segregate us from each other and from God.

Several days before this first sermon, several deacons had told me that black people were not welcome. Yet on Sunday I preached about love, the love that Jesus showed, a love that embraced all people. I made it clear that anyone coming into the sanctuary would not be stopped. After the service was over, I stood at the back door greeting the people; one deacon (a white gentleman) said, "I know what point you were trying to make–but I still love you anyway."

It seemed as if the most remote, insensitive hearts might belong to those already sitting in the pews.

And yet today—even as a yellow pad on my desk lists my desire to be used in the reconciliation between blacks and whites under the title, "The Fourteen Things I Hope to Accomplish Before I Die"—I have seen how African-American and Asian pastors in Philadelphia recently confessed to their racism and then broke down weeping. I've seen pride broken, sins confessed, and lives restored in the most insensitive hearts, in the most unlikely parts of the country. I believe these incidents are God's notes on his yellow pad—giving us a peek at the coming revival.

I know our God is moving. This book will tell you how I know.

Chapter One:

Ordinary People Living Quiet, Anonymous Lives—Until . . .

All over this nation, God is moving people to pray and preparing them for a unique touch of His hand. Already we are seeing amazing breakthroughs in areas that once seemed cold, indifferent, and even antagonistic to the Gospel. *Something* is definitely happening.

Chapter Two:

What is Happening to Our World?

Does the continuing moral, social and spiritual decay in the United States raise more fear than hope inside you? Could you and I be part of the problem?

Yet the news is not all bad. In our discouragement we discover what God requires of us and what happens to a people when they ignore Him. In every national downturn, a small group of individuals is able to see through the darkness. What makes these people different is that they have already seen what's at the root of their country's woe—sin. Through their joy you will see how far our nation has drifted from God.

Chapter Three:
A Truth We Almost Forgot

At least four times in our nation's history the prevailing cloud of darkness has been pierced by heaven-sent revival. The results were strikingly similar to what we're witnessing today: God raised up chosen leaders, then prompted personal brokenness leading to confession, prayer, a thirst for holiness, evangelism, and a desire to rebuild society. The other similarity? It seems God never works the same way twice! No one knows specifically what this emerging spiritual awakening will look like. Still, the parallels to the past are too obvious to ignore.

Chapter Four:
When Broken, Humbled People Come Together

Imminent awakening is not a collection of solitary spiritual journeys but a movement of God that transforms whole communities, from those persons who sit in pews to those serving on city councils. Not only does God's light revive individuals, at the same time He renews *the means* by which they come together. When you see how this comes about, you'll appreciate why people are admitting, "Only God could do this. . . ."

Chapter Five:
Why Prayer is the Key

Prayer is the single clearest expression of the new awakening taking place today. And it has ignited some powerful waves of personal renewal and national awakening, beginning with the most unlikely regions in North America. I was privileged to see such an event as it touched hundreds of church leaders.

Chapter Six:
Unseen Obstacles Up Ahead

In our excitement to capture and sustain renewal, we can be tempted to package and franchise the movement. This awareness has brought Christian leaders to their knees (again), aware that human pride and non-godly forces could disrupt a holy work in progress.

Chapter Seven:
What Will the New Awakening Look Like?

Like past spiritual awakenings, America's next great renewal will yield positive social improvements *only* insofar as they are rooted in godly convictions. This is not a warning, but a reality. Christians can and must lead the call to serve our nation's needy.

Chapter Eight:
The Most Important Decision of All

Revival has broken out throughout our nation when people have turned to God in godly repentance and humility, weeping over and asking forgiveness for their sins and their selfish lives. This is spiritual awakening—to be a true follower of Christ living in a continual state of revival as a clean vessel for His service. To get a grasp of God in Spirit and in Truth, and then live it, is to know revival.

This is the most important decision of all: will you choose to seek Him, to love Him and to follow Him? Are you open to the new awakening God wants to bring about in *you*?

Epilogue:
Preparing for Personal Revival

What does all of this mean to you? A helpful series of questions will help you examine your own life.

Where's the Fire?

Is a fresh revival ready to sweep across this nation? Could God really be about to ignite a holy fire that could kindle the hearts of millions with a holy passion for Himself and His kingdom? While I believe the answer is yes, I know one thing for sure: God sees beyond our crippling human condition to the new life in Christ He desires for every person. Take the example I saw on the infield of Jack Murphy Stadium in San Diego several years ago.

We had reached the conclusion of a Billy Graham Crusade and a powerful testimony was being given. I had already heard her story: Wife of a pro basketball player, divorced and hurting. Then she turned to drugs and became one of satan's prized examples of how people build their own prison with chemicals–until Christ set her free. She described how others could also find the freedom she now enjoyed. After the crusade I received a one-page letter with these three lines:

> Me full of heroin.
> Pockets full of heroin.
> And I went forward to receive Jesus.

The writer, Raul Gonzales, had been a drug addict living on a diet of pills and powder until his self-punishment became too great. After he met Christ he returned to the people who had managed to survive his real-life nightmare. For the past twenty years Raul and his group, Teen Challenge, in Hartford, Connecticut, have led pimps and pushers to a Carpenter from Nazareth who has helped them rebuild their lives. "We are seeing revival in our cities," says Raul. "It is happening with people who have nothing but Christ."[1]

Should I have been surprised that one as humble as Raul saw the first crack of light of a new national awakening? Should I be surprised that God works through the weak, the poor, the unlikely? No. And yet, somehow, I still am.

How many times did the subject of faith come up with my "church member" brother-in-law, Art Bailey? How many times had he politely declined to discuss his own spiritual condition? Ten? Twenty? I lost count after the first dozen conversations. I remember the morning he and his wife came home early from a trip; I had been house-sitting for them. I was kneeling by the side of my bed when the bedroom door opened. Art came in and found me on my knees, weeping.

"What's going on, Tom?"

It was then I told him the story of how I had been praying for him to be forgiven and that he might know Jesus as Lord and Savior. Art looked at me and said, "No one has ever wept for me before." Then he began to cry—the tears of a heart overcome, but not those of one's actually receiving Christ.

Art and I had more conversations. Then, several months later, a diminutive, seventy-two-year-old ex-boxer friend of Art's became the catalyst for the greatest reversal Art would ever know: he gave his life to the Person he had so long ignored.

As a new Christian, Art began devouring the Bible. After a year of intensive discipleship training, Art and another friend (whom he had introduced to Christ) began a weekly morning meeting every Tuesday at 5:30 A.M. to study the Bible, to make the Word their own, and to pray. How Art had changed! The only thing he wanted was to get to know this God intimately, and for others to be stirred to new life by the Lord who had revived his own heart.

Since the early 1970s, as a result of his own personal awakening, Art has given his life to the work of evangelism in the Philippines and other developing countries. Today his prayer is that this country, his native United States, would experience a national change of heart, a rekindling of purpose and direction fanned into flame by deep-felt confession and convicting prayer.

If a national awakening is on the horizon—if, in fact, a revival has begun to dawn, as more and more people believe it has—I believe it is because people—pastors, desperate heroin addicts and seekers alike—come face-to-face with their undeniable need for a personal relationship with God that can only be found through Jesus Christ. In people such as these I see a God who can heal our land in a way that could touch every corner of economic and social need.

This God, who has worked in history to bring people to Himself, is again making history in our time. From Pastors' Prayer Summits to huge national youth gatherings; from prayer concerts that attract hundreds at a time to hundreds of prayer meetings in America's high schools and small inner-city churches; the God of the Bible—the God who is working in extraordinary ways in our nation—is alive in ways we never expected. As you stand back and see what He is doing, I believe you will find Him irresistible. The thought of remaining a spectator will become less and less appealing.

When your curiosity gives way to awe, when your awe gives way to concerted prayer that takes you to the foot of God, your own renewal will have already begun. This will be the start of your spiritual renewal, the unpredictable result of an undeniable Lord who is now awakening our nation, one life at a time.

Endnotes

1. Raul Gonzalez, telephone conversation, 4 February 1994.

CHAPTER ONE

Ordinary People Living Quiet, Anonymous Lives——Until . . .

Something of potentially historic proportion is bursting out all across the United States. While it may not yet be front page news, a growing number of individuals and churches are convinced it is happening. And now both their stories and the evidence of this emerging explosion have begun to leak out.

If it had been just an isolated incident or two, I probably would have discarded the events of the past ten years in a file marked "Coincidence." But as more facts have surfaced, some undeniable patterns have emerged. In fact, I believe that what I and others across this nation are now seeing is not a series of random events, but an emerging phenomenon that is alive, true, and too wonderful to ignore.

At a small downtown community church in Memphis, Tennessee, thirty-five men gather for a special Saturday morning meeting. They have learned that a man in their congregation, whose marriage is now crumbling, has been seeing another woman. Opinion in the room ranges from judgment to confusion. As the pastor prepares to launch the discussion, the agenda hits a snag. The man in question stands up.

"I have something I want to say," he declares. "After our thirteen-year marriage, my wife decided to leave. For the past several months, I've been seeing a woman. Some of you know her. Lately we've been spending more and more time together. There has been no sexual involvement between us." The man's voice begins to break, and he begins to weep.

"I've done everything I can to try restore my marriage, but it hasn't worked. I hope none of you ever has to go through what I've experienced in the past couple of years. I know that what I've been doing is wrong. I'm sorry. I ask you to forgive me."

The pastor, who has talked to the man nearly every day during his two-and-a-half-year ordeal, puts his arms around him. He hugs him and as he begins to cry with him, he says, "Bill, I love you, and I forgive you."

For a moment, Bill and his pastor are oblivious to the other wet eyes in the room. Suddenly, another man stands up to speak.

"I did not come here to do this, but there's something I have to say. I have lusted after women for years. Women in this church. Women you know. I need your forgiveness—and God's."

He sits down and another man stands up and clears his throat. "I can no longer hold inside me what I feel. I've carried feelings of hatred toward some of you in this room. I've become a bitter man. I can't go on. I need to stop, because it's wrong, it's sin."

Before the morning is over, twenty other men speak up and confess their own sins. Weeks later, these same men start a monthly gathering to pray for the church and each other. It is the first time such a thing has taken place in the church's short, eighteen-year history.[1]

In Portland, Oregon, the pastor of a large church attends an inaugural Prayer Summit with forty-five other pastors from the Portland area. As he sits in the evening communion service, he is privately skeptical about what could really happen between a group of pastors from different denominations. As a Pentecostal, he is aware of the lingering animosity between his denomination and some of the area's Conservative Baptists.

After communion, a fellow pastor whom he does not know comes up to the communion table and addresses the group. "I want to confess, tonight, that I stand here as a part of the Conservative Baptists in Portland, and I ask forgiveness of my Pentecostal brothers who are here. I feel we've done more than any other group in the city to quench the Spirit of God. If there is a Pentecostal brother willing to stand here at the communion table with me, I'd count it a privilege."

Moments later, the Baptist pastor is joined at the communion table by a Foursquare pastor, his pentecostal counterpart. This man—whom he had never met—says, with humility and grace, "Not only do I accept that apology, I want to offer an apology on behalf of the pentecostal church for the arrogance and pride that somehow projects an attitude of superiority." Through the event, the two men become close friends and agree to pray together every Wednesday morning.[2]

In Philadelphia, 120 pastors come together for a similar weekend of spontaneous worship and prayer. During the first two days, a number of African-American ministers approach the event's facilitators with the same request: "You've got to bring up the racial issue. We need to pray about the racial issue."

"We don't bring up anything because we're not directing anything," replies one of the organizers. "The Holy Spirit brings up whatever we're led to pray about."

That evening, during a worship service, the pastors are invited to approach the communion table on their own as they feel ready. With no prompting, an Asian pastor gets up from his chair, slumps onto the floor, and begins to cry: "God, forgive me of my sin of racism toward my black brothers." Immediately a dozen African-American pastors come forward and surround the man. They hug him and begin to offer prayers for him. While this continues, one of the pastors slips off to the side of the altar where he kneels. His head bowed, he begins to whisper, "God, forgive me for my sin of racism toward my Asian brothers."

The communion service continues for hours. The next morning the pastors tell the facilitator, "This was the greatest breakthrough in the city of Philadelphia in a hundred years."[3]

A *few months later*, the same organizer returns home from a similar weekend retreat with pastors. Once inside the door, his wife asks, "How did the Prayer Summit go?"

The man tries to talk but can't. Instead he begins to weep. Later he tells his wife, "Every word that I could think of is so grossly inadequate to describe what it was like to be in the presence of God. It is unlike anything I have ever seen in my lifetime. Brokenness over sin among church leaders, the tremendous joy of sins being forgiven, the awesome presence of Christ—all of these things are character traits of revival."[4]

Several miles away in the same city, a high school student is one of fifty-one hundred church members who fast and pray for all or part of the week. During that time, the young man intercedes daily for his friends at school. On Monday while at lunch in the cafeteria, he opens his Bible and begins to read. Immediately he is surrounded by a dozen friends who begin to ask questions about Christianity. That night he goes to a social function and, again, is surrounded by fellow students who are curious to know more about the Bible and Jesus Christ. While he has always been open about his faith, the boy admits, "I've never seen students my age so curious about the Gospel. And it all happened right after I fasted and prayed."[5]

In Oklahoma City, a successful real estate developer admits, "Our nation is in trouble today. We are experiencing a spiritual hunger. People today want to know about Christ more than Christians want to tell them about Him."

The man's next-door neighbor was one such person who had shown little interest in anything of a spiritual nature. In fact, for years the two said few words to each other. When the next-door neighbor began to make false, public accusations about the developer over a business matter, communication became nil.

Several years later, the neighbor was rushed to the hospital with a stroke that kept him bed-ridden. A year later his wife died. One day during a subsequent hospitalization, he looked up to see the developer, his neighbor, standing at his bedside. Shock gave way to awkward greetings. For the next hour and a half, the conversation meandered from IV bottles to loneliness and finally to God. The developer listened as his bed-ridden neighbor began to spill out his need. The discussion led to a prayer and the man accepted Jesus Christ as his Lord and Savior.[6]

A Native American pastor from Vancouver, Washington, sits among three hundred people from forty-three countries at an international conference on spiritual warfare. At one point in the general session, a Christian man, a Caucasian, stands up and asks him for forgiveness on behalf of all Caucasian people for the injustices they have committed against the Native people of the United States. The Native American forgives him and then asks forgiveness on behalf of Native people "for the bitterness, resentment and even hatred that many of our people feel toward white people." The event triggers new, unanticipated acts of reconciliation between peoples from South Africa to Japan. The pastor admits, "All of us wept and then rejoiced as we witnessed this incredible move of the Spirit in the areas of repentance and reconciliation for racial and national sins."[7]

In Long Beach, California, nine thousand junior and senior high and college-age youth gather on New Year's Eve—not for a rock concert, but for the chance to study the Bible. The event has tripled in attendance in just three years and draws youth from nine foreign countries and throughout the United States.[8]

In Anaheim, California, a crowd of fifty-two thousand men meets at Anaheim Stadium to worship and pray at one of seven national conferences for a growing ministry to men called Promise Keepers. The group's promotional brochure contains these words: "America's moral foundation is crumbling today under the weight of broken promises. This pressure is shattering marriages and families, and creating widespread hurt, pain and unrest. Times are changing, however. A sovereign move of God's Spirit is stirring the hearts of men to become men of integrity, promise keepers."[9] One attendee said, "The Holy Spirit filled our hearts, breaking our willfulness and transforming us into real men; men who will get on their knees and pray with and for their wives. . . ."[10]

In Dix Hills, New York, an attorney who has just returned from a week of fasting and prayer stands up in a gathering of local clergy and lay Christians who have been meeting to talk about possible follow-up steps after the Long Island Billy Graham Crusade.

"I think we need a plan of prayer," the man says. "We need to pray before we evangelize." The attorney then holds up a map of Long Island and urges the group to begin praying for their region. From that day on, the format of the meetings changes from lunch and discussion to fasting and prayer. The group mails out a monthly invitation with a newly declared mission statement:

Long Island Prayer Fellowship is a group of Christian church ministry and business leaders who come together to pray for repentance and revival in our land. We sense the call of God to set aside doctrinal and denominational differences and proclaim the Lordship of Jesus Christ and the unity of the Body of Christ. To further this end, we have made commitments of prayer, fellowship and dynamic evangelism. We pledge ourselves to seek a deeper unity and truth, worship, holiness and mission. We believe that only our prayer, repentance and seeking God will bring healing to this land and we purpose to give ourselves to that goal.

Within weeks, the head of a local minister's group writes back: "A clerk in a Christian bookstore told one of our women, 'I believe something is happening on Long Island. I can tell by the books people are buying.'

"I believe God is doing something, also," the pastor continues, "and I want to be involved in it."[11]

Something So New and Wonderful, No Words Can Explain

Today, I too believe God is doing something in our nation, and I want to be involved in it. I share this conviction with men and women who are part of the early stirrings of a major spiritual renewal going on right now in the United States. In prayer groups, pastors' conferences, worship services, men's gatherings and a host of other settings from Philadelphia, Pennsylvania, to Portland, Oregon, Christians whose denominational, ethnic and economic borders have broken down are saying the same thing. Put a stethoscope to the collective heart of men and women who have been stirred, and you will hear a common response: "We are experiencing something so new and wonderful that no words can explain it. And it is out of our control. Quite simply, we have beheld the Lord, and we will never be the same again."

I have written this book not so that you would marvel at a movement, but that you would be drawn to the Lord. The striking evidence of God's life and love in everyday people cannot be denied. As you step closer to catch a glimpse of this new spiritual awakening, the reality dawns: God is using a relatively small handful of broken, humbled people to draw individuals, communities and an entire nation to Himself. As you read, I believe your curiosity will give way to a genuine awe and attraction to the God who is as real and present as your own breath. The question, *Is this spiritual awakening for real?* will have been replaced by a new desire: *How can I know this God and be a part of what He's doing in my world?*

When this happens, you will be nearing the heart of the movement: God's greatest desire, as the Supreme Evangelist, has always been for individuals to know Him personally. Today, the disparity between His perfect will and His imperfect people has set the stage for unavoidable and historic consequences.

For too many years, the pipeline God has chosen to reach the rest of the world—you and me—has been gathering rust. The pipes have become clogged. We have been content to go on living, aware that things are not quite right, yet too lazy to do much about it.

If we really believed God was serious about wanting to flow through His Church, we shouldn't have been surprised that He first needed to clean out the rust! It was there all along for us to read: "Therefore if anyone cleanses himself from these, he will be a vessel for honor, sanctified and useful for the Master, prepared for every good work" (2 Timothy 2:21).

In other words, purging must occur before the Holy Spirit can flow into our nation, our churches, our lives.

Today, the first trickles of rust have begun to break loose and flow from the vessels of our lives. The persons you just met know the pain and promise that awaits others. Their conviction, confession and turning to Christ are the initial fruit of the Holy Spirit that could carry us toward the first major spiritual awakening in the United States in more than 130 years.

What Awaits Us?

As I have talked about such a possibility with church audiences throughout North America, there is no shortage of questions:

> *How have we arrived at this moment of spiritual hunger and renewal in our country?*
>
> *How can I know it is real? How is this movement different from other spiritual awakenings that have swept across our country?*
>
> *How can I believe there's a spiritual renewal going on if I don't see any evidence of it—especially when I'm being bombarded by so much news of violence, abuse, gangs and moral decay?*
>
> *How can spiritual renewal bring about lasting change? Our church seems so dead!*

Often, by the end of a presentation, the mood of mild skepticism has bubbled over into extreme interest and excited comment.

> *When you explained Charles Finney's seven indicators of spiritual renewal that have been present in every major awakening in the United States, I realized that at least the first three are already present in our country. Is it just a matter of time before the next four become apparent?*
>
> *I never knew there were biblical examples of how God may usher in a national spiritual awakening in our own day. When I look at people like Hezekiah in the Old Testament, I can see the parallels to our day.*
>
> *You've described how when God moves, He changes whole churches, even whole cities, in a way that*

impacts nations. If this movement continues to grow, what could it mean for our nation?

How can I move from being a spectator of what God is doing to becoming a participant? I want Him to awaken me!

When I hear comments such as these, I am more and more convinced that the violence and unrest darkening our nation should not be confused with the possibility that the house lights have dimmed in anticipation of the curtain going up on history. Christians who were once comfortable as spectators have discovered they're actually part of the script.

If you believe it's possible that God can work through ordinary people—if you've seen prayers answered and lives changed by the one, true Savior you know to be Jesus Christ—this book is for you. Even if you find yourself standing on the fringes of faith, I believe you may find your own footprints strikingly similar to those left by the men and women whose journeys fill these next few pages.

Is God's Spirit Sweeping Through Your Own Life?

Are you willing to be surprised by God? Are you open to the possibility that your very human wounds of unrest, anger and pain can be avenues of healing? They can; I know. You will find God's fingerprints all over the people in this book who considered themselves to be the most unlikely means for God's love to flow into this world.

And that includes a man who had grown content with his own rust, Tom Phillips. Just when I am struck by the depth of our nation's sin, I see my own rust: "Lord, I am filled with pride. There is more inside me that needs to be cleansed. I, too, need to wake up from my own human tendency to slumber. I, too, need a forgiving Jesus so I can approach a perfect, all-loving God."

In my own moments of purging, I have gotten off my knees a more humbled, more broken man. I admit that I am a member of a church that has become corroded and impure, a church that God loves and wants to renew in what Richard Owen Roberts has so succinctly and accurately defined as "an extraordinary movement of the Holy Spirit producing extraordinary results."[12]

Every time I have had to face myself and my inadequacy, I have returned to an ancient promise: "If my people who are called by my name, will humble themselves, and pray and seek My face, and turn from their wicked ways, then will I hear from heaven, and will forgive their sin and heal their land" (2 Chronicles 7:14).

If these words are still true, then you and I have the chance to be part of a movement of God that could well bring about the spiritual, social and economic transformation that our country so desperately needs.

Who will take part in this movement? My growing belief, confirmed by the past twenty-two years of study, conversations and observations, is that He often works *through people who are already seeking Him.*

Regardless of how near or far you find yourself from God, my hope is that this book will kick-start—if not fuel—your own desire to know Him intimately. Your moment of personal renewal with God can happen at any time along our journey.

Endnotes

1. Larry Baskin, telephone conversation, 27 January 1994.

2. Tom Baker, telephone conversation, 1 February 1994.

3. Terry Dirks, telephone conversation, 4 February 1994.

4. Ibid.

5. Tom Baker, telephone conversation, 1 February, 1994.

6. Warr, Gene, telephone conversation, 25 January, 1994.

7. Richard Twiss, telephone conversation, 2 February, 1994.

8. Tom Baker, telephone conversation, 1 February, 1994.

9. Promise Keepers, "Seize the Moment," promotional brochure, 1994.

10. Ibid.

11. Larry Mancini, telephone conversation, 1 February, 1994.

12. Richard Owen Roberts, *Revival* (Wheaton, Illinois: Tyndale House Publishers, Inc., 1985), 6.

CHAPTER TWO

What Is Happening to Our World?

It started out as a little, innocent comment. One woman raised her hand, then came the question everyone was thinking, yet no one had asked. Without knowing it, she had identified *the* issue, the one undeniable possibility I had puzzled over for years.

It all happened one morning several years ago while I was speaking at a church in Rochester, New York. The topic was church revival. For the previous four months I had given the same presentation to church audiences of just about every denominational stripe throughout the country. I wasn't merely comfortable with the message; I had become shaped by it.

"Today, there is growing evidence to suggest that we in North America could be on the threshold of a major spiritual awakening," I said. And with that I launched into a carefully orchestrated outline of Scripture, complete with historical context, personal observations and overhead transparencies on how a new, emerging spiritual awakening in the United States was real and eminent. After forty-five minutes I finally took my first breath. Then I opened it up for questions.

That's when she raised her hand.

This middle-aged woman stood up and said, "Tom, I appreciate what you've said so far about the need for spiritual renewal in our country. I believe God has poured out his Spirit in extraordinary ways on different people at different points in history. I just don't buy the idea that we're in one of those times. And I'll tell you why.

"When I look around me, I see so much darkness. Families divorcing. Young lives being ripped apart by drugs, sex, and drive-by shootings. The neighborhood, the city, the country I grew up in just doesn't exist anymore. Face it, you don't see people smile as much as they used to. Look at our world. It's filled with angry drivers, ugly graffiti and one major world disaster after another. Starving people, bankrupt governments and hurting friends. That's why, if you're talking about the possibility of spiritual renewal, well—it's just wishful thinking, if you ask me. How can spiritual awakening be anything more than that when the one thing Christians can't wait to get home for after Sunday service isn't to pray or study God's Word, but to worship the Dallas Cowboys?"

Out of the corner of my eye I could see people nodding their heads, perhaps the same way you're nodding yes right now. "America, on the verge of another Great Awakening, Tom? How could that possibly be when things around us are in such a mess?"

At first glance, I would have to agree. If God is doing something extraordinary to transform the hearts and minds of Americans, you sure wouldn't know about it from the news:

- In Dartmouth, Massachusetts, three schoolboys surround a classmate and stab him to death–then laugh and trade high fives.[1]

- In Oakland, California, a teenager brandishing a knife chases a woman down the street while onlookers chant, "Kill her! Kill her!"[2]

- Members of Hamilton Square Baptist Church in San Francisco attending their Sunday evening service on September 19, 1993, are attacked by radical gay activists. The church is surrounded by more than a hundred rioters who scream and rough up parishioners attempting to enter the church. When protesters try to break through the doors and gain forcible entry, boys and girls inside the church begin to cry. Later, after seeing youngsters inside, protesters pound on the glass and shout, "We want your children, give us your children." A nine-year-old boy cries, "They are after me. It's me they want." The pastor, Dr. David Innes, begs for additional police support, but the request is denied. He's told, "You must understand, this is San

Francisco." No arrests are made.[3]

- In Lakewood, California, members of a high school gang named "Spur Posse" are accused of raping and exploiting hundreds of girls as young as ten. One of the members, Eric Richardson, says to a reporter: "They pass out condoms, teach sex education, and pregnancy-this and pregnancy-that. But they don't teach us any rules."[4]

Gang violence. Abortion. Promiscuity rampant among teens and now creeping into elementary school. These are all symptoms of the same sickness in our culture, a profound lack of regard for the sanctity of life. Without a moral code that calls us to nurture and protect people, it's no wonder that a frightening new anarchy has spilled over into the hallways and classrooms of our schools. *U.S. News & World Report* estimates that more than three million crimes a year are committed in or near the nation's eighty-five thousand public schools. A University of Michigan study reports that 9 percent of eighth-graders carry a gun, knife or club to school at least once a month. In all, an estimated two-hundred-seventy-thousand guns go to school every day.[5] "It used to be," says United States Senator Barbara Boxer, "that our children feared the shoving and pushing of the class bully. Now all too many of them worry about the Uzi that he might have in his locker."[6]

At the 1994 National Prayer Breakfast in Washington, D.C., a small woman in a blue and white sari steps to the podium. Though the gathered religious and political leaders can barely see her head, her words paint a devastating and unavoidable picture. "The greatest destroyer of peace today is abortion, because it is a war against the child, a direct killing of the innocent child, murder by the mother herself," declares Mother Teresa. "And if we accept that a mother can kill even her own child, how can we tell other people not to kill one another?"[7]

How indeed? On another front, back home from a trip to Bosnia where thousands have died from months of bloody ethnic fighting, Franklin Graham writes, "I was in the city of Mostar as it was being shelled. I met with the Minister of Interior in his office as bombs exploded outside. As we talked he described to me a shocking videotape he had just seen—it showed eleven soldiers raping a nine-year-old girl, murdering her father and brother in front of her and then dismembering her body."[8]

But the evil, of course, isn't limited to small Balkan countries. On the Fox Network television comedy "Married with Children," one episode featured:

- A man who had watched porno movies while walking around, bent over with an erection;
- Two men pretending to fondle nude mannequins, and;
- A male stripper taking off his clothes down to a G-string.[9]

If reports like these aren't enough to suggest that the prospect of spiritual renewal is little more than wishful thinking, along come the latest sobering numbers that confirm what many have known all along: our nation is in deep trouble.

- In one year alone, a sixteen-year-old child sees more than fifteen thousand sexual acts and references on TV. By the time they reach high school, children have witnessed thirty-three thousand TV murders and two-hundred thousand acts of violence.[10]
- Former Secretary of Education Bill Bennett's "Index of Leading Cultural Indicators" finds that since 1960, violent crime became a top concern of Americans and illegitimate births climbed by 419 percent.[11]
- And don't look now, but America's mushrooming promiscuity has entered the church. A study conducted by Josh McDowell reveals that 43 percent of teenagers attending evangelical or fundamental churches have engaged in sexual intercourse by age nineteen.[12]

After reading all this, I wouldn't be a bit surprised if you shared the frustration of the woman who stood up that morning in the church seminar. To her, America is no closer to a sweeping transformation of God's Spirit than the North Pole is to Miami Beach. No wonder she and so many Christians today believe "The best days are behind us. From here on out, it's only going to get worse." For some, the bad news is more than headlines; it's the sign that we've reached a new era.

Charles Colson has said on many occasions that we

are now living in a post-Christian culture. If he means we're a people destined for a life after God, then we would truly have reason to despair (ignoring, of course, the biblical promise that all that He does within us is according to *His* power, Ephesians 3:20). I would guess that most Christians today edge close to the view of Billy Graham. Although in 1974 Mr. Graham thought we would see another major revival in our country, ten years later he told me that he didn't see a spiritual awakening on the horizon. Instead he saw gangs, murder and drugs—not good, but evil. He believed there might never be another international spiritual awakening because of such evil.

Living Amidst Darkness and Light

The question I asked Mr. Graham next is the same one I want to ask you: Is it possible that the next major spiritual awakening could be different? Is it possible that evil and good will continue to grow, because the Bible promises there will be a climax of both at Armageddon?

Today both Mr. Graham and I agree the answer is yes. Let me be very clear: the darkness in our world today is not about to overcome God's light, rather it is merely a backdrop for things to come. At the 1995 National Prayer Breakfast in Washington, D.C., Mr. Graham noted in his evening plenary address that the February 6, 1995, issue of *Newsweek* magazine was titled, "SHAME, How Do We Bring Back a Sense of Right and Wrong?" Mr. Graham noted that even a secular news magazine was calling America to repentance and crying out that our nation needs a spiritual and moral awakening.

The early signs of spiritual awakening in our country are a mere pinpoint of light in a darkening landscape, a pinpoint of light that can be seen only when everything else is black—a pinpoint of light whose gleaming presence is a brilliant reminder that darkness has never been able to overcome light. This conviction is illustrated for me in a frightening experience I had as a teenager.

When I was eighteen, my friend Clay Crockett and I decided to explore a cave near the Tennessee River. We entered the tunnel with the bravado of Indiana Jones. After walking twenty minutes or so, all signs of natural light had vanished behind us. This wasn't a problem until our flashlight died. Clay claimed he knew the path back out. I wanted to believe him. Oh, how I wanted to believe him! I could feel the sweat bead up on the back of my neck as I held up my hand in front of my face . . . but saw nothing.

There was only blackness. And thick, dank air.

I tried to picture the gray rock walls I had seen just a few minutes before, but I couldn't. I tried to visualize the path, the turns we had taken. I tried to see it all in reverse, groping for some kind of mental road map that would get us both out. Yet when I turned my head, I saw nothing—only a deep, impenetrable blackness. I panicked that I had lost my sight. All I could hold on to were sounds—my heartbeat, my breathing, the sterile echo of my shoes as they inched across bare rock. Finally I knelt down; Clay did the same. It was the only thing we could do. We knew what was up ahead.

We should have been able to walk out, but there was one thing somewhere in our path we couldn't see, something we knew existed but couldn't pinpoint: a dry well thirty feet deep and six feet across. One missed step, and one or both of us would plunge to certain injury or even death. The only way out was to crawl. Me, "walking" on my hands and knees, checking the ground inch-by-inch. Clay behind, walking stooped, holding on to my belt. Ten minutes. Twenty minutes. With sharp edges of rock digging into my kneecaps, I lost track of time. Since we simply backed up and retraced our route, I had to believe we were going in the right direction. Belief was all we had; our eyes were wide open, yet our world was pitch black.

I don't recall which of us saw it first—a speck of something white. It was light, smaller than a dust particle. And yet it was huge, because it meant we were headed in the right direction! There *was* a way out of the cave, and we were on that one and only path.

This is how I believe the coming spiritual awakening will occur, by defining the lines of darkness and light. The contrasts will be so sharp, the evidence of the Lord so clear, that no world leader, no movement, no organization or coalition will be able to take credit for such an obvious spiritual transformation. Like people lost in a cave surrounded by darkness, we will know that there can only be one explanation: God Himself!

What we're seeing in the United States today—a return to prayer, confession and a new spiritual hunger—is more than a mere pinprick. It is God's light shining in the hearts of His people, the Church. Much like Creation "when the earth was formless and empty (and) darkness was over the surface of the deep . . . " (Genesis 1:2), God is at work again, not dispelling darkness, but piercing it.

How will we be able to see this? How will we be able to realize that God is working not only in the midst of darkness to revive Christians with renewed life, but also through such a revival to bring new life to those who are yet to believe? We know it because this is the promise of Psalm 67:2: "May your ways be known on earth, your salvation among all nations."

God's constant re-creative nature to rekindle His people, and through them to light that same fire in others who have only known darkness, is undeniable and ready to emerge again in our time. The question is, "Will we choose to be part of it?" More basic than this is, "Will we be able to recognize such a renewal as it unfolds before us?"

The imminent revival I'm talking about is so different and so radically life-transforming—so unlike the world we live in today—that the only way to see this spiritual movement is with a new set of eyes different from the ones you and I were given at birth. It's only with spiritual eyes able to spot and follow a pinprick of light that you and I will be able to see beyond this present darkness. Only when we know this truth will we understand the necessary reason and seize the undeniable hope for seeing that this current speck of God's light is much bigger, much brighter, than our world's current darkness.

As I have already suggested, today's emerging national revival is a movement that knows no geographic or demographic boundaries. Joe Aldrich, president of Multnomah Bible College and Biblical Seminary and the founder of International Renewal Ministries, has seen God's extraordinary work at a Pastor's Prayer Summit near Portland, Oregon, where ministers, many weeping, openly confessed their sins to each other. David Bryant, head of Concerts of Prayer International, has seen the Lord bring together between six- and seven-thousand youth in Cleveland for city-wide prayer rallies. Every leader I've talked to has reaffirmed that "something new and powerful from God is going on in America." Each of them also can point his or her own moment of spiritual awakening.

I know what it's like to be lost in a cave. But there's a second personal experience that's integral to my understanding of revival. It has to do with being humbled, with broken pride. My appreciation for personal revival and its relationship with national spiritual awakening has to do with being blind to God and being able to see Him with new, spiritual eyes.

The Essence of Revival: A Personal Story

For me, a major turning point took place on a painful afternoon in Asheville, North Carolina, in 1988. Up to that time, my life had been filled with accomplishment and praise. The day my personal pride crumbled was the day I started to see God's extraordinary character, in some ways for the first time.

I grew up in the farmland of northern Mississippi in a loving Christian family. My dad was a soldier, then a carpenter. Eventually he owned half a dozen businesses, including a gas station. When I was eight years old—the same year I became a Christian—he had the best help a father could hope for, an eager son who was willing to do almost anything he asked. If a customer rolled in with a dirty windshield, I'd wash it. If my uncles—who picked cotton all day in the hot sun—were hungry and thirsty, I took them lunch and a gallon jug of ice water wrapped in old newspaper. I was obedient. I never remember lying. I never smoked nor drank (except for a sip of warm beer when I was ten, which was the last time I touched the bottle!).

When I was twelve our family moved to the city, and I became a nobody. My pants were too small and tight, my shirt "uncool." The best conversations I had were with myself. Books became my best friends and my nickname became "Encyclopedia." With the help of a college scholarship I was going on to medical school. But two years into my studies I couldn't ignore a question that had been hounding me. Finally, one night it caught up to me: "What's more important: saving a life so that a person can live another seventy or eighty years on earth, or helping save a soul for eternity?" In a stairway of a friend's apartment I fell to my knees and began to weep. I had heard my calling. My heart was tied to helping people know God's love.

In 1975 I began working with Billy Graham. I directed evangelistic crusades in the United States and Europe and oversaw efforts in counseling and follow-up. Never in my life had I faced such fulfilling and demanding work. Thankfully, there was a spiritual mentor, Charlie Riggs, who guided me through the rapids and torrents that inevitably came. With the staff I eventually guided and served I sought to dispense the credit to others rather than claim it for myself. My management philosophy was not "me," but "we." In fact, for a long period of time I wouldn't write a letter with "I" in it.

Yet I had my flaws. I knew I had a large ego. Awareness finally came when I was perched at the highest level of responsibility I had ever attained. I was to be director of a new center to train and send evangelists throughout the world. All of my study, training and ministry had prepared me for this moment. Then, as soon as my vision began to come together, the whole thing began to unravel. Mixed messages from various people, responsibilities not clarified, expectations not met, all conspired to undo the situation.

Everything I had prepared for, worked for, lived for in ministry was not to be. Not in this "opportunity."

That's when a gray sense of despair began to press in. Against my nature I took pills to help me sleep, but they did no good. I was Mr. Obedient and, against my character, I wanted out, out of the religious politics that had always engulfed others, out of the compromising character of others. On a few terribly lonely nights I thought I wanted out of life, not because I wanted to commit suicide, but because I wanted to be with Christ—someone who was perfect, pure and loved me unconditionally.

On that painful afternoon in 1988, three thousand miles from my wife and family, I sat by myself in a small hotel room. The pressure to make good on my ministry commitment, knowing I wasn't wanted or valued, refused to go away. Stress quickly became depression. It came not from the outside, but from within, attaching itself to my soul like a bloated leech—a terrible, dark feeling without bottom or end.

I remember the exact moment my panic reached its peak. I rushed over to the only window in the room thinking, *What am I going to do?* I looked outside. I had to see something that was alive, something that could break through my darkness. I gazed through the window but there was no one in sight—just vegetation, a hillside with bushes, and a tree. Praise God for that single tree! As I saw the wind rustle through its upper leaves, I saw *life*.

I must have stared at it for a long time, for at that moment, surrounded by the blackness within me, this tree was the only living thing I knew. Without warning, the picture changed. A bird flew toward the tree and lightly perched on one of its top branches. Immediately, something happened inside me.

For the first time in days, perhaps weeks, I felt life surging within me. Life unexpectedly trickled back into my black world. I thanked God for this tiny bird because through it I was seeing life overcome death in me. I knew I couldn't stop looking until all the mental blackness went away. After three or four minutes of silence, of praying and trusting God, the blackness faded.

A month and a half later I resigned my position. I had accomplished what I had been asked to do. Outwardly it was a cordial departure; inside, I felt terribly wounded. If you've ever been moved aside, let go, passed over or simply ignored—and you know you've done all the right things that were humanly possible at the time—then you know the kind of circumstance I'm describing. In your mind it can all make sense, but nothing, it seems, can take away the hurt.

For years I had prayed, "God, make me like Christ." For years I had been so confident. I was the clay on the potter's wheel, so sure that I was going to be molded into positions of greater and greater responsibility; after all, I knew, with Him, I couldn't fail. And yet I had. Why? Why would this God I had served and loved for so many years want to break me?

> "O house of Israel, can I not do with you as this potter does?" declares the LORD. "Like clay in the hand of the potter, so are you in my hand, O house of Israel" (Jeremiah 18:6).

I knew the Scripture. Since I knew clay didn't control the potter's wheel, I could only do one thing: pray to the Master Potter that He might mold me to be more like Christ. For years He had been working to shape my character, so flawed by prideful imperfections I couldn't see. So why would God allow me to be broken at the height of my ministry career? Why would He push down the clay of my life and remold me?

The only answer I can give is that I had prayed to be a vessel, His vessel (2 Timothy 2:21). For years—through seminary, in early churches I pastored and through global evangelistic efforts—I had been lifted up by others, only to find that the vessel did not control the potter. While being grateful to God, I was still proud of the vessel. I remained unconscious of a deeper truth going on at the time. All I saw were immediate benefits and the next logical rung on the ladder of my résumé. I couldn't see the hairline cracks in my own character. Had I stepped into the fire of the new position I wanted so badly, the vessel that God had spent years shaping would have been blown apart.

And so in His own way, God did a very loving thing. He allowed me to go through a severe breaking. He cut short my dream so that His will could be fulfilled. He could have made the correction silently and painlessly so I wouldn't have felt a thing. (That would have been my choice!) However—and here's His great patience and love at work—He allowed the process to be turbulent enough so that I was forced to sit up and take notice. He allowed me to feel my self-satisfied ego and other personality flaws being crushed.

Alone with myself, I cried.

Alone with the sight of a simple tree, I began to live.

Alone with God, I saw the wisdom of the Master Potter. He didn't take me off the wheel and give up on me!

Because of that dark day in Asheville, I once more rejoiced in ministry. I got in touch with my most obvious flaws. And I confessed them before God, not knowing that my own personal revival had begun.

Striking Similarities to Our Nation

What does the forming, breaking and reshaping of clay pots have to do with spiritual awakening in America? Everything! Especially if you ask the pastors and laypersons you'll meet in the following pages. Is their spiritual transformation incidental, random, without national significance? Or is there more going on? Look at places like Portland, Oregon; Memphis,

Tennessee; Long Island, New York; and other communities across the United States where God has begun to bring revival to His people, and you'll see some striking similarities.

In each community, these Christians demonstrated a new *commitment to pray* and trust God for what He wanted to reveal to both them and their churches.

In each fellowship, *confession of personal and corporate sin* triggered the expressed desire for God's forgiveness, leading to reconciliation among fellow Christians and a sweet unity in worship.

In each gathering, the outward expression of personal brokenness and a renewed will to obey and serve God preceded *an extraordinary movement of God's Spirit* that knew no human explanation. Such movements are occurring today in pockets all across our nation.

There is much more to say about each of these three common characteristics—prayer, confession of personal sin and the extraordinary spiritual results to which they ultimately lead.

Whether you believe a major spiritual awakening is imminent or merely a remote possibility at best, it's hard to deny that God is drawing His people to Himself and that His people are poised to reach others with Christ. There's hope for those in spiritual darkness.

If the current flicker of God's light leads to a widespread spiritual awakening in this country, will we look back and realize God began His work through unlikely individuals who were simply broken and humbled? Isn't it interesting that personal humility has always been a prerequisite of major Christian leaders and the movements their faith has inspired?

- Dietrich Bonhoeffer, scribbling a diary of costly discipleship in a dim German jail, knew that his execution was only days away.
- Martin Luther King, Jr., resisted a life of demeaning slurs and the fire hoses of angry whites with non-violent love.
- Mother Teresa, living a quiet discipline of poverty in a Hungarian convent, prepared herself for the day she would pick up the first of some twenty-six thousand beggars from the gutters of Calcutta.

Each leader was humiliated, emptied of self and brought to the admission that "I *have* nothing, because before You I *am* nothing. Therefore anything I own, anything I do, anything I hope to become, can come only from God alone."

Isn't it interesting that in these three classic examples, we see God using broken people who live and work in the midst of needy and (in some cases) desperate surroundings? *If a major spiritual awakening does takes place in our country, will it be because God makes His will known, not in the absence of evil's influence, but in the midst of an ever-darkening world?*

- Before 1988, few Christians in Portland held out much hope that area pastors could ever reconcile their long and bitter denominational disputes.

How humorous (and how like God) that a model for pastoral reconciliation and renewal would spring up in Oregon, a state that's home to the nation's highest proportion of people without a God-based value system!

- A church in Memphis, where spiritual awakening has stirred, grew out of an inner-city mission to the down-and-out. Sixty-five percent of the church's original members came out of alcohol- and drug-related backgrounds. See with me the tears of a man in Memphis who confessed to adultery. Do you think the elders in that Saturday breakfast meeting would have admitted their own shortcomings had their leader not said what he did? Hardly. Can their tearful confessions bring others to their knees, and through their weakness allow them to seek the only One they ignored? Absolutely.

Is this the kind of light that's piercing the dark conscience of our nation, a country in which we find abortion on demand, rising teen suicide, AIDS and a national debt that some say is synonymous with an inevitable economic collapse? Referring to a poll by the Family Research Council in December 1993 that showed United States citizens favoring traditional values by a margin of 76 percent to 19 percent, James Dobson writes, "How can such wholesome developments occur in the midst of almost unprecedented wickedness? Isn't that what Scripture teaches us?

Romans 5:20 says, 'But where sin abounded, grace did much more abound.' "[13]

This analysis is certainly true today. As the culture moves away from its Judeo-Christian roots, more and more people appear to recognize the devastation of sin and are turning to the Good News of the Gospel. They cry out to be saved from themselves and be secure in Christ.

While I don't see swells of revival sweeping across our country, I do see something nearly as significant: pockets of broken, humble people in less-than-perfect conditions who, both individually and corporately, are beginning to experience the fullness of God in ways most believers of our nation have never approached. Their willingness to pray, to confess their sins to each other and to the Lord, and to remain in awe of God alone as the author of this new movement, is exactly what the Lord had in mind when he made His famous promise to Solomon:

> If my people, who are called by my name, will humble themselves and pray and seek my face and turn from their wicked ways, then I will hear from heaven and will forgive their sin and will heal their land. *Now my eyes will be open and my ears attentive to the prayers offered in this place* (2 Chronicles 7:14-15, italics mine).

In a word, this is God's desire both for Solomon's era and for our own. He longs for us to experience a true, personal, spiritual awakening. I don't mean a pre-planned sawdust-trail event, but an awakening in the fullest meaning of the word—"revival," which in the Old Testament meant "to wake up and live."

Who today wouldn't want this? Who wouldn't want to see beyond the evil in our nation, to know revival as Robert Coleman has described it so infectiously: "breathing in the breath of God"?

Already you have met several people who are now experiencing this new life. And you will meet others. As you see their documented experiences of how God broke through their desperate situations with near-indescribable power, the word "revival" may begin to take on new meaning. You will learn what few Christians today realize—that a new commitment to prayer, public confession and a humble awe of God has preceded every major revival in corporate, regional or national America. It's all in the record.

When you read about the crime, moral unraveling and spiritual deadness that led up to those long-ago spiritual movements, you'll think historians have stolen the newspaper off your front porch. But that would be impossible, wouldn't it?

. . . Almost as unlikely as history repeating itself in our time.

Endnotes

1. Charles Colson, *Christianity Today*, 7 March 1994, 80.

2. Ibid.

3. David Innes, telephone conversation, 24 January 1995.

4. Jane Gross, "Where Boys Will Be Boys and Adults are Bewildered," *The New York Times*, 29 March, 1A.

5. Bruce Frankel, "Our Problem Cuts Across All Groups," *USA Today*, 8 December 1993, 3A.

6. "Praying for an end to a wave of fear," *U.S. News & World Report*, 4 April 1994, 4.

7. Mother Teresa, EP News Service, 11 February 1994, 3.

8. Franklin Graham, letter to constituents, Samaritan's Purse, July, 1993, 2.

9. Terry Rakolta, newsletter, *Americans for Responsible Television*, 1994.

10. Ibid.

11. Ibid.

12. Mark Graham, "Sex and the Nazarene Teen," *Herald of Holiness*, May 1993, 47.

13. James Dobson, January letter to constituents (Colorado Springs: Focus on the Family, 1994).

CHAPTER THREE

A Truth
We Almost Forgot

Look around your neighborhood. On the surface, nothing seems to have changed much in the past several years. The streets look the same; so do the houses. Sure, there's more congestion, but that's what you would expect with growth.

Yet appearances can be deceptive. Remember when you used to take a nice evening walk? Those days are gone. They ended when the crime you had been reading about for years began to invade *your* neighborhood. Now, the news of random break-ins has been pushed aside by other, larger, growing threats: loss of confidence in government, global economic instability, despair of "Generation X," and the still-unresolved potential epidemic called AIDS.

These hazards typify the cries and groans of a deeper national sickness that has left our country in a moral deep-sleep. Everyone knows it, yet few people do anything about it. Why? We just feel hopeless.

In such a climate you might think that churches would be growing—and a few are—but many long-standing denominations are losing members. Giving is down. Operational budgets and mission programs are hurting. The same people who smile and shake the pastor's hand at the door see society unraveling before their eyes with no turnaround in sight. All the things that could ignite hope for positive change—the Bible, prayer, Sunday worship—are labeled irrelevant and lifeless by outsiders looking in. They not only question Christianity, they hold the church in contempt. On the other end of the national landscape, Christians look at a morally adrift, self-centered culture and ask, "How far can all this go?"

It's Happened Before

You might be surprised to learn that Americans were asking just such a question . . . in 1794! If you think our current moral decay, increasing violence and crumbling ethics are signs of an inevitable, darker downward spiral, think again. Consider the uneasy twilight of the late eighteenth century. Illegitimate births were rampant. Alcohol, the drug of the day, was destroying families and wrecking futures. Thomas Paine was proclaiming that Christianity was dead—and certainly, the body of faith appeared to be in a coma.

Yet even as church rolls were shrinking and greed, sensuality and family breakdown were becoming more widespread, America was about to experience a great spiritual revival.

It would start small, in a handful of broken-down corners of society, with a few people praying. In one year it would spread like a wildfire through churches, seminaries and families, changing the spiritual landscape of entire cities and towns. People would spend days and nights in prayer and worship. Christians who believed God had given up on their nation saw thousands of people admit they were dead inside and find new life through forgiveness wrapped up in a power they had never seen before. This phenomenon would unfold for the next forty-five years. And though it was the first time America had experienced revival, it would not be the last.

How do we make sense of the growing evidence that our country and our continent could be ripe for a major spiritual awakening? Evangelist Bob Cryder has suggested, "If revival happens in the sanctuary (and we're beginning to see isolated cases), then we're standing in the foyer." Today an increasing number of Christians, including myself, believe we're *that* close.

Four times in history, God's Spirit of revival has touched our nation and transformed its people. The elements that led to each movement bear a strange resemblance to events that have now taken place as the twilight of the twentieth century gives way to the dawn of a new millennium.

Now—as then—Christian leaders are being brought to their knees through humble, public confession.

Around the United States, in a growing number of pockets, prayer is exploding. People of all economic, racial and denominational hues are turning back to God. Clearly, the spiritual hunger of our day offers conspicuous clues to historic parallels that cannot be denied. It is time we looked at:

- The unique, yet strangely similar, qualities of America's major revivals that parallel what's currently going on in individual lives, churches, prayer groups and homes.

- The amazing consistency in the blessings that revival produced in Old Testament times; the same blessings our nation so desperately needs today.

- The seven indicators that reveal not so much how close or far away we may be from experiencing revival, but how God is now calling people to Himself.

Let's look more closely at each of these points. Let's resist the temptation to forecast when or if revival will happen in our country. Instead, let's spend a moment with history. If our spiritual eyes are open, we may begin to see what God is doing in our land. And as we begin to look, let's pray a prayer patterned after some wise men from the tribe of Issachar: "Oh, God, make us men and women who understand the times so that we may know what we ought to do" (1 Chronicles 12:32).

The Great Awakening

You don't have to listen too hard to make out the cries of harried, suburban Americans in the late 1990s. Pressed by too many demands, too little time, mushrooming pressures and shrinking paychecks, people are quick to confess, "I'm just trying to survive." That's exactly what Americans were saying in the days that led to our nation's first Great Awakening. Forced with building a society from scratch, the early settlers defined the word "pressure." Pressure didn't come from daily freeway commutes or seventy-hour work weeks, but from fighting medical emergencies without 9-1-1 and winters without cozy, insulated homes. Crops failed, diseases spread and early deaths were common.

Where was the Church in all of this? In 1606, the First Charter of Virginia articulated the deeply held Christian principles of our nation's founders:

> We, greatly commending, and graciously accepting of, their Desires for the Furtherance of so noble a Work, which may, by the Providence of Almighty God, hereafter tend to the Glory of His Divine Majesty, in propagating of Christian Religion to such People, as yet live in Darkness and miserable Ignorance of the true Knowledge and Worship of God, and may in time bring the Infidels and Savages, living in those Parts, to human Civility, and to a settled and quiet Government.[1]

By the century's end, however, something had been lost. Thanks to the Halfway Covenant, a person could belong to a church without believing in Jesus Christ for salvation. The Halfway Covenant allowed unbelieving children of believing parents to receive baptism; they simply weren't allowed to receive the Lord's Supper or vote on church matters. Thus was faith reduced to a formality. People lived with growing irreverence, succumbed to rampant dishonesty and grew reluctant to acknowledge the word "sin."

Jonathan Edwards, perhaps the greatest theologian our country has ever produced, "lamented the deterioration of society. He wrote that even 'children were given to night waking and tavern haunting.' "[2]

Into such a dismal cultural climate a spiritual outbreak occurred which no one could have predicted—the Great Awakening. On one Sunday, Theodore J. Frelinghuysen, a twenty-nine-year-old Pietist, preached what few wanted to admit: human beings were depraved and needed a personal encounter with God and a change of heart. But it was Edwards' preaching that reverberated in the hearts and minds of his hearers. When he asked his congregation, "How many kinds of wickedness are there?" he didn't wait for a response; he simply described what he saw all around him: irreverence in God's house, disregard of the Sabbath, neglect of family prayer, disobedience to parents, quarreling, greediness, sensuality and hatred of one's neighbor.[3]

Edwards had the holy nerve to weave his accurate assessment into a gripping word picture that showed people they were as helpless to do anything about their own sinful condition as insects dangling over an open flame: "You hang by a slender thread, with the flames of divine wrath flashing about it, and ready every moment to singe and burn it asunder; and you have nothing to lay hold of to save yourself, nothing to keep off the flames of wrath, nothing of your own, nothing that you have ever done, nothing that you can do to induce God to spare you one moment."[4]

The effect of Edwards' sermon set New England ablaze. Men and women wept tears of deep remorse. They knew they needed to be forgiven. They came to God on their knees and out of their deep sorrow they received an unexpected feeling of cleansing and joy. What was dead came to life.

Revival had come to America.

Spiritual night was nailed beneath the floor of spiritual dawn. The new fervor spread to a hundred communities. Nearly three hundred people—25 percent of eleven hundred individuals in his town alone—were then converted. The Great Awakening witnessed an immediate, overt transformation in men and women throughout New England. People felt deep conviction when they realized they had turned their backs on God. Guilt led to confession, confession led to forgiveness, and forgiveness led to new devotion to a Savior thousands had never known.

By 1735, The Great Awakening began to cool. It might have ended altogether had it not been for George Whitefield. If Edwards was the spark of revival, Whitefield became the flame that forced the movement to spread. In thirty-two years in the mid-1700s, this Englishman made seven trips to America to preach. His style was dramatic and pointed. "I love those who thunder out the word," he said. "The Christian world is in a dead sleep. Nothing but a loud voice can awaken them out of it."[5]

By 1760, few were still asleep. During The Great Awakening, 150 Congregational churches were founded and an estimated twenty-five to fifty thousand people became believers—as much as 14 percent of New England's total population of 340,000. Today, using the most conservative figure, that would be like seeing every person in New York, Chicago, Los Angeles, Houston, Philadelphia, San Diego, Detroit and Dallas decide to live for Jesus Christ. When the Church was revived, the salvation of thousands of unregenerate sinners followed.

By the time the flame of The Great Awakening began to die out for good in 1760, thousands of people who once had turned their back on God had changed their way of living. From New England to the colony of Jamestown, where the people's indifference to the Bible had been strong, conversions to Christ were so remarkable it was agreed that only God could have brought about such a sweeping transformation. To some, the revival must have seemed total and final. Never again would they face such desperate spiritual poverty. Never again, they believed, could things get so bad.

In a way, they were right. Forty years later, the situation would be even worse.

The Second Great Awakening

By 1800 the American church was in trouble again. The Revolutionary War had inflicted serious damage on believing communities. Scores of congregations that had sided with the British had lost their prestige. Others were scattered and many of those still intact had been left without pastors. In a war fought, in part, to protect religious freedom, church buildings had been dismantled or used as barracks or stables.

The real casualties were the people. Worship waned and immorality flourished. As the survivalist mentality moved westward into Appalachia, spiritual basics of Bible reading and prayer were left behind. Colleges such as Yale, Princeton, and William and Mary—centers of learning that had been founded on Christian belief—now disowned their charters.

Orthodox faith was swept aside by rationalism. In the mind of Thomas Jefferson and other influential thinkers, reason left no room for a Creator intimately involved with people. To the deist, God had wound up the universe and put the clock in our hands. If an individual or society grew, it wasn't because God guided, intervened or empowered; it was because people exercised their rational, human minds. Rationalism's rise made faith a white elephant. The results were devastating. Episcopalian Devereaux Jarret wrote, "The state of religion is gloomy and distressing; the church of Christ seems to have sunk very low."[6] Kenneth Scott Latorette, the great church historian, proclaimed, "It seemed as if Christianity were about to be ushered out of the affairs of men."[7] And United States Chief Justice John Marshall wrote this obituary: "The church is too far gone ever to be redeemed."[8]

Yet the bleak moral and spiritual outlook became a blessing in disguise. Christians felt so low there was nowhere to look but up. Baptist minister Isaac Backus said, "There's only one power on earth that commands the power of heaven—prayer."[9] In 1794 he mailed letters pleading with pastors to set aside the first Monday of each month to pray. The response was overwhelming. Within a short time, Baptists, Presbyterians, Congregationalists, Reformed and Moravians were joined in a national movement of prayer. In Ohio, Kentucky and Tennessee, prayer groups also sprang up.

Rationally speaking, nothing should have come from it, especially in places like Logan County, Kentucky. This sordid haven for criminals, robbers and vigilantes lived up to its name: Rogue's Harbor. While constantly praying for spiritual awakening to shake the town, a Presbyterian minister named James McGready conducted a community-wide communion service in 1800. Later that year he held another Lord's Supper over a weekend and eleven thousand people flocked to the tiny Gasper River Presbyterian Church. Some came from as far as one hundred miles away. With nowhere to stay, the crowds slept outside in tents, bed rolls and covered wagons. "No one seemed to wish to go home," wrote McGready. "Persons of every description, white and black, were to be found in every part of the multitude crying out for mercy in the most extreme distress."[10]

In McGready's *Narrative*, Barton W. Stone, a follower of the pastor, described what he saw: "There on the edge of the prairie, multitudes came together. . . . The scene was new and strange. It baffled description. Many, very many fell down as men slain in battle, and continued for hours together in an apparently breathless and motionless state. . . ."[11]

It was only a prelude to what took place one year later in Cane Ridge, Kentucky, where some ten- to twenty-five thousand men, women and children gathered to worship and pray. The gathering was so large, yet so united, that four to five preachers, standing on stumps of recently hewn trees, spoke at the same time. Denominational differences melted into a display of emotion that had never before been seen. One person present said that eight hundred persons "were struck down," laying incoherent on the ground for minutes, even hours.[12] James Finley, who later became a circuit rider, described the sound "like the roar of Niagara. . . . At one time I saw at least five hundred swept down in a moment as if a battery of a thousand guns had been opened upon them, and then immediately followed shrieks and shouts that rent the very heavens."[13]

When George Baxter, President of Washington College in Virginia, rode through the same region of Kentucky some months later, he called it "the most moral place I have ever seen. . . . A religious awe seemed to pervade the country. . . . Upon the whole, I think the revival in Kentucky the most extraordinary that has ever visited the church of Christ. . . . Infidelity was triumphant, and religion was on the point of expiring. Something extraordinary seemed necessary to arrest the attention of a giddy people who were ready to conclude that Christianity was a fable. . . . This revival has done it! It has confounded infidelity, awed vice into sitting and brought numbers beyond calculation under serious impression."[14]

The facts bore this out. On the sparsely populated frontiers of our country, the number of Methodist

Wesleyan believers increased almost fivefold from twenty-seven hundred to twelve thousand. From 1799 to 1803, an estimated ten thousand people joined the Baptist church. The revival gave birth to a new interest in missions and organizations such as the American Bible Society and the American Sunday School Union.

By its very name, The Second Great Awakening proved that revival could happen again. If evangelism was an ongoing command, revival was a periodic movement meant to bring a nation back into a right relationship with God. Some at the time concluded that revival—the presence and power of Christ that gives a person meaning, direction, purpose and hungering for more of God—was (and is) a return to normal Christianity. (I also believe this.) Though its context and expression were vastly different from the spiritual revolution of Edwards' and Whitefield's day, the revival of 1800 startled thousands of families, churches and Christian leaders out of their spiritual slumber. They came to the same conclusion that had once sustained their spiritual ancestors—in the midst of a nation's darkness, those who know they're lost will be able to see the pinhole of light that leads to God.

If The Great Awakening responded to a lack of truth, the Second Great Awakening corrected the untruth of skeptical rationalism. Cane Ridge showed that God can change a community overnight. The real story was not emotionalism *per se*. The real story was that the dramatic outpouring of remorse, confession and faith matched the depth of a previously hardened people's longing for a God they had abandoned. The Second Great Awakening showed that regardless of how far a nation had drifted from God, God could breathe new life into repentant people and revive their nation. America's new spirit of Christian devotion was so strong, some thought it would never end. But then, these people were not living in the city where a third Great Awakening was about to take place.

The Great Prayer Revival of 1857-59

The following observations have been made about the United States. Can you name the year?

- Gambling, gain and greed are widespread, with a rapid increase in violent crime.

- The occult dominates in a nation hungry for the supernatural. Spiritism has gained a popular foothold over many minds.

- A playboy philosophy of "free love" is advocated and accepted by many.

- Commercial and political corruption is epidemic. Bribes, graft and illegal business practices are rife in the nation.

- Atheism, agnosticism, apathy and indifference to God, to the church and its message are omnipresent. The decline is fourfold: social, moral, political and spiritual.[15]

This was how Dr. J. Edwin Orr described America in the 1850s. It was this depraved culture that swirled outside the third story of an old church building in New York City where Jeremiah Lanphier invited people to join him for a noon prayer meeting. Lanphier canvassed the downtown corridor for weeks inviting people to come to this gathering. On the big day, Thursday, September 23, no one had arrived by 12:30 P.M. By one o'clock six people had showed up. This was enough encouragement for him to decide to hold a second meeting. The next Wednesday, twenty people came. The third week there were forty.

Then, on October 14, the worst financial crisis in the nation's history hit. Banks closed their doors. People lost their jobs. Families went hungry. And at Lanphier's Fulton Street meeting, more than three thousand people crowded in to pray. Six months later, ten thousand businessmen in New York City were gathering in groups for daily prayer.

Over the next two years, one million people throughout the United States—one-thirtieth of the entire population—committed themselves to Jesus Christ. The Fulton Street Revival changed the lives of physicians, lawyers, accountants and scores of other men and women and their families.

Only one explanation has ever been given for such phenomenal spiritual impact: prayer. Prayer was what a layman named Jeremiah Lanphier knew would reach God. Prayer was what drew the first trickle of people to his third-floor office. Prayer was what caused hundreds and thousands of people, many who had never seen the inside of a church, to fall to their knees. Prayer was what inspired newspaper headlines to shout:

City's Biggest Church Packed Twice Daily for Prayer
— New Haven, Connecticut

Business Shuts Down for Hour Each Day;
Everybody Prays
— Bethel, Connecticut

State Legislators Get Down on Knees
— Albany, New York

Ice on the Mohawk Broken for Baptisms
— Schenectady, New York

Five Prayer Meetings Go Round the Clock
— Washington, D.C.

Revival Sweeps Yale
— New Haven, Connecticut[16]

The Great Prayer Revival of 1857-59, like the First and Second Great Awakenings, was unique. Unlike either movement before it, the revival Lanphier sparked was almost totally led by lay people, began and flourished throughout all denominations, and relied on united prayer. Yet despite all their uniqueness, look at what all three Great Awakenings show us about revival:

We can't predict it.

We can't plan it.

We can't shape it.

We can only trust that when our nation reaches a point of spiritual, moral and social no-return—as it appeared to do at least three distinct times in history— an extraordinary movement of God's Spirit may move in extraordinary ways. Every time God has moved in such a way in our country, He has done so through the simple confession, brokenness and obedience of individuals. This is totally consistent with how God always seems to bring His people back to Himself.

The Revival in Judah

The story of King Hezekiah provides a clear, biblical example of how revival blesses a nation through the faithfulness of one person. Seven hundred years before the birth of Christ may seem light years away from today—until you read Hezekiah's description of his society.

> Our fathers were unfaithful; they did evil in the eyes of the Lord our God and forsook him. They turned their faces away from the Lord's dwelling place and turned their backs on him (2 Chronicles 29:6).

Less than one month into his reign, Hezekiah called his people to restore the temple as they restored a new relationship with God. "My sons," he said, "do not be negligent now, for the Lord has chosen you to stand before him and serve him, to minister before him and to burn incense" (2 Chronicles 29:11).

For years the Jews had been living in a dark time of instability and apostasy. The nation that once had walked in the ways of God scraped by as a derelict collection of disorganized, disoriented and disenchanted people. In many ways they were just like their previous ruler, King Ahaz, who ignored, rebelled against and walked away from God. Yet through the faith of one man, King Hezekiah, their long march of disobedience and drought ended. (Imagine reclaiming your own house of worship after it had been condemned by years of indifference and spiritual decay.)

Through the vision, courage and faith of one person, a nation began to return to God. The call of Hezekiah resulted in a revival in which "the whole assembly bowed in worship, while the singers sang and the trumpeters played" (2 Chronicles 29:28).

Worship was just the beginning. Something truly remarkable happened that had not taken place in generations; believers called upon each other to repent (2 Chronicles 30:6). The call brought new unity (2 Chronicles 30:12) and a new desire among the people to give a greater portion of their earthly treasures back to God (2 Chronicles 31:12). Individual renewal grew into a tremendous corporate response as people shared their material possessions with others in need (2 Chronicles 31:19). What began as humble confession became a movement of national repentance, obedience and meaningful social change.

This is exactly what happened in each of our country's three Great Awakenings. When a nation's darkness becomes overwhelmingly destructive, only God can supply what people need to be brought back to life. These things include the assurance of being forgiven, accepted and loved; the joy of worshiping God alone; and a return to holy living. When God brings revival to a nation, He blesses His people with a call to return to five specific commitments:

1. The authority of the Scriptures;

2. Belief in the centrality of the Cross;

3. Increased devotional life and return to personal holiness;

4. Explosive witnessing and discipleship, and;

5. Corporate social change that results from individual, spiritual transformation.

Does seeing the embryonic development of one or more of these things mean our nation is one step closer to revival?

In my view, this is the wrong question to ask. Trying to predict any movement of God's Spirit is impossible—and even harmful. We could be so caught up in wanting to know "When will it happen?" that we lose an appreciation for how consistent God's expression of love is in revival. The great thing about seeing how God has revived our nation three times in our history (and how He revived His covenant people in Scripture) is that we see God's consistent character and blessing at work.

Though the means of each revival were unique to each time, people and place, God's results were resoundingly clear. The attraction of these timeless results isn't that they help us *predict* revival (they can't), but rather that they cause us to *long* for revival. When you see what marvelous things God has done through revival, you can't help but ask, "What if?"

> *What if God were to move through our land in a way that caused people to admit they could no longer go on with their broken, unhappy lives?*
>
> *What if people turned from their self-centered greed, prejudice, hatred and violence?*
>
> *What if the change was so obvious, so far beyond explanation, that people everywhere freely announced, "This could only come from God!*

Imagine what would happen if true revival visited our nation once more:

- The Bible would return to company board rooms, schools, legislative halls and homes of people who know it's *the* authoritative source for living.

- A new understanding of the Cross of Jesus Christ would sweep the land. People would relearn how much we deserved to die, what Christ did in our place and the value of the resurrection.

- Widespread prayer and worship would be embraced by people who bring to their workplaces, classrooms and homes a kind of love that makes people put away their mistrust, fear and dislike for one another.

- Christians would freely and openly share Jesus with people who not only accept Christ, but hunger to know God through an amazing resurgence of study and prayer.

- Cities and towns would be transformed by group after group of Christians who cause an astounded public to admit, "Never has this city seen such compassion and love that truly works."

It's ironic that the man who reconfirmed these realities in the midst of America's Second Great Awakening was a legendary evangelist who believed there was nothing miraculous about revival, that spiritual awakening was not so much God's intervention but the inevitable, unquestioned result of people's obedience. Though rationalism was the enemy of faith, it's interesting that Charles Finney used his God-given gifts of rational insight and reasoning to communicate the need for revival.

Charles Finney

Charles Finney was born in 1792 and reared with little Christian influence. As a young student of law in Adams, New York, he attended church and even sang in the choir as an unbeliever to improve his law practice. Yet, since so much of law in his day was based upon Scripture, Finney was forced to consult the Bible on a regular basis. This tall, angular member of the New York Bar Association made sure his reference Bible was hidden under other books on his desk so that others wouldn't see it. Before the concept of revival ever entered his mind—while he debated with himself whether to give his life to God—the authority of Scripture became all too real. Walking back to his office one autumn day, Finney heard a voice he could not deny: "Will you accept it now, today?" After moments of soul searching, Finney remembered the words of Scripture: "Then shall ye seek me and find me, when ye shall search for me with all your heart." He cried out, "Lord, I take Thee at Thy Word."[17]

The authority of Scripture and the conviction that sin could be eradicated in a person's life only through the cross of Jesus Christ—the very things he would one day preach to thousands—changed Finney's life. He described his dramatic moment of conversion "like a wave of electricity going through me. . . . I could not express it in any other way. It seemed like the very breath of God."[18]

The very next day Finney shouted his joy to all who would listen. Twenty-four people did so and gave their lives to Christ.[19] In his *Memoirs*, Finney records how his new relationship with Christ radically changed his profession as a lawyer the first day after his conversion:

> Deacon B—came into the office and said to me, "Mr. Finney, do you recollect that my case is to be tried at ten o'clock this morning? I suppose you are ready?" I had been retained to attend this suit as his attorney. I replied to him, "Deacon B—, I have a retainer from the Lord Jesus Christ to plead his cause, and I cannot plead yours."

Finney's single-minded determination showed in his own increased devotional life and personal holiness. Finney refused to attend seminary and adopt others' concepts of Scripture. He chose, instead, to study the Bible himself. He developed what he called "Measures," or principles; if a Christian applied them, he believed God had to respond.

Wherever Finney preached throughout western New York, crowds turned out. Almost always, true revival broke out. Almost without exception, people who heard Finney's sermons broke out into confessing their sins, repentance and weeping. During one historic, six-month preaching tour in Rochester, New York, a hundred thousand people gave their lives to Christ. In Boston, fifty thousand decisions were counted during the week Finney preached. And once when Finney was speaking in Philadelphia, a group of lumbermen who heard him returned as spiritual ambassadors to the woods where no schools, churches or pastors existed. During the next year, five thousand people in their community came to Christ.

Many disagreed with Finney's personal preaching style. While most preachers talked about "the sins of others," Finney addressed his audiences directly. "What will you do with Jesus Christ?" Finney always demanded a verdict on this all-important issue. Many of those converted went on to exert a profound social impact in their day.[20]

Like Hezekiah before him and Lanphier to follow, Finney saw the mark of true revival: Christians with the power to change society because their inner beings had changed. Their actions were the overflow of God's undeniable love, which they could no longer keep to themselves.

Finney's "Seven Indicators"

Finney couldn't know at the time that he was living in the last period of spiritual awakening our country has seen until now. How ironic, then, that he would write his "Seven Indicators" of coming revival. He used his brilliant human intellect to help us understand how God's infinite Holy Spirit breathes life into a nation. Finney was not interested in forecasting history, yet—130 years after they were written—Finney's indicators may cause us to think again about extraordinary expressions of the Holy Spirit in our nation that have already caused many to say, "I had no idea these things were happening."

What are these "Seven Indicators" and what can they tell us about how God is moving today?

Allow me to list them for you and to ask a question: How many Americans today do you think would agree with Finney that revival is coming . . .

1. When the sovereignty of God indicates that revival is near.

2. When wickedness grieves and humbles Christians.

3. When there is a spirit of prayer for revival.

4. When the attention of ministers is directed toward revival and spiritual awakening.

5. When Christians confess their sins one to another.

6. When Christians are willing to make the sacrifices necessary to carry out the new movement of God's Spirit.

7. When the ministers and laity are willing for God to promote spiritual awakening by whatever instrument he pleases.[21]

How many of these seven indicators would you say are real and present where you live and worship? One? Two? Five? How many have you already seen reported in the newspaper or heard about from a friend in church? Let's take a closer look at four of these seven indicators.

When wickedness grieves and humbles Christians.

Thousands in Seattle expressed outrage and compassion when they learned that a baby's body had been found one morning in a city garbage dump. Did you ever think you would see the day when thousands of Christian youth would show their outrage against today's rampant premarital sex by "planting" 211,000 individual, personal pledges to preserve sex for marriage on the Mall in front of the Washington Monument?

When there is a spirit of prayer for revival.

Concerts of Prayer International reported that forty-five hundred churches and forty-two thousand individual Christians were involved in concerts of prayer through forty city-wide tours throughout the United

States in 1991—a 100 percent increase over 1990.[22] And this is just one ministry.

In San Diego, quarterly prayer meetings have drawn twenty-five hundred Christians in response to the words of Jeremiah to "Seek the peace of the city, wherein I have called you to go captive, and pray unto the Lord for it. For in its peace you too shall find peace" (Jeremiah 29:7). As a result, according to the Reverend Mike MacIntosh, pastor of Horizon Christian Fellowship in San Diego, the city's crime rate went down in the next twelve months, churches that focused on Jesus Christ have grown and evangelism has flourished.[23]

When the attention of ministers is directed toward revival and spiritual awakening.

Churches in 140 cities across North America have held Pastors' Prayer Summits through International Renewal Ministries of Portland, Oregon. As of January 1995, another 180 Pastors' Prayer Summits were either confirmed or being considered.[24]

When Christians confess their sins one to another.

The words of Dr. Joe Aldrich, President of Multnomah Bible College and Biblical Seminary, are not just wishful thinking but an accurate description of what is now taking place in congregations across the country: "In this movement we're watching today, there is a desire to see God really impact a community. But to *impact* a community, we must *be* a community. To be a community, we must have unity. To have unity we must have humility, and to have humility we must rediscover holiness."[25]

People such as Larry Mancini in Bayshore, New York; Terry Dirks in Portland, Oregon; and Art Bailey in Atlanta, Georgia, are making this painful, life-changing discovery. Their stories suggest that revival is both "now" and "not yet." Humility, prayer and confession are here-and-now realities. Are Christians willing to make the sacrifices necessary to carry out revival? Are ministers and laity really willing for God to promote spiritual awakening by whatever instrument He pleases? The evidence suggests "not yet", but soon.

If A New Day Is Dawning . . .

The reason Finney's seven observations are worth examining is that they describe the personal revival of Christians in pockets of our country. While I've met or spoken with each of the people you've just met, one other person stands out as a special example of what revival can mean in one person's life.

I met Shawn Wilkins at Central Church in Memphis, Tennessee. He agreed to serve as a leader for the upcoming Billy Graham Crusade. Slowly, in small bits, he revealed his story. His father had been a professional gambler, a freewheeling character who won and lost millions of dollars. At twenty-four, Shawn became one of the youngest, most successful brokers for a leading brokerage firm. He did all the normal things he thought were part of growing up. He got married, had two children and in a very short time became financially successful. As long as no one found out what he did after work, listened in on his phone calls or checked his appointment calendar, he was fine.

Shawn's life of secrecy ended on March 23, 1975. He found himself sitting in large arena listening to a man on stage talk about the Bible. Six months earlier he had accepted the Bible, accepted the God-in-a-manger story about a Savior coming to earth and dying on a cross for him. But the words he prayed at the time hadn't changed what he did in his free time. The man at the lectern began to speak about family, a father's responsibility, and the relationship with:

his own earthly father . . .

Listen to your father, who gave you life, and do not despise your mother when she is old. . . . The father of a righteous man has great joy; he who has a wise son delights in him (Proverbs 23:22, 24).

his own children . . .

Fathers, do not exasperate your children; instead, bring them up in the training and instruction of the Lord (Ephesians 6:4).

his heavenly Father . . .

As a father has compassion on his children, so the Lord has compassion on those who fear him" (Psalm 103:13).

Shawn could only listen. And think:

This guy knows me.

This guy is speaking exactly to the things in my life.

For the first time, he faced it all in the silence of his own heart—everything he didn't like about himself, everything he had kept hidden from his wife, Jana Lee, everything he could hide in a daily marijuana habit and relationships his wife knew nothing about.

At the end of the four-night series, Shawn took the words he had mouthed before, wrapped them up in what little faith he had, and let them rest in his heart. And then the speaker challenged Shawn to do something that was totally impossible, to read his Bible every day from this day on. "If you make this vow and don't fulfill it," the speaker said, "it will be like a millstone around your neck."

That was nearly twenty years ago. In all but about thirty of the past 7,300 days, Shawn has chosen to have his life shaped by the wisdom and truth of God's Word. Today Shawn Wilkins' personal Great Awakening is still in progress. What happened to our nation as a result of revivals is still unfolding in his life—brokenness, confession and a new, total dependence on prayer. The man I met back in 1977 bears little resemblance to the devoted husband and father I know today. He is a walking definition of revival, because in Shawn Wilkins, God "brought back to life that which was dead."

If a new revival is dawning in America, I believe I may already have caught a glimpse of what it looks like in Shawn and many others across our nation. If a

Fourth Great Awakening is yet to come, it may look like what has already begun to unfold in Portland, Oregon; Long Island, New York; and Memphis, Tennessee. The more I've listened to people tell their still-unfolding stories, the more I've become intrigued by the striking similarities of our nation's past and present-day turbulence.

Should the gatherings of public confession and corporate prayer in churches across our country be called merely isolated events? Or is something greater going on? Is this "something else" a new, dramatic unfolding of God's plan?

The only way to know is to sit back and listen to the stories, seeing His work in others with the eyes of a man or woman of Issachar. And let the evidence speak for itself.

Endnotes

1. *The Rebirth of America* (Niles, Michigan: Arthur S. DeMoss Foundation, 1986), 46.

2. Mary Stewart Relfe, *Cure of All Ills* (Montgomery, Alabama: League of Prayer, 1988), 19.

3. *America's Great Revivals* (Minneapolis: Bethany Fellowship, Inc.), 10.

4. Ibid., 13.

5. Ibid., 14.

6. J. Edwin Orr, "The Role of Prayer."

7. Ibid.

8. Ibid.

9. Mary Stewart Relfe, *Cure of All Ills* (Montgomery, Alabama: League of Prayer, 1988), 27.

10. James McGready, *A Short Narrative of the Revival in Logan County, Kentucky*.

11. Ibid.

12. *America's Great Revivals* (Minneapolis: Bethany Fellowship, Inc.) 41.

13. Ibid.

14. Mary Stewart Relfe, *Cure of All Ills* (Montgomery, Alabama: League of Prayer, 1988), 34.

15. Ibid., 40-42.

6. *America's Great Revivals* (Minneapolis: Bethany Fellowship, Inc.) 64.

17. Ibid., 76.

18. Ibid., 77.

19. *The Rebirth of America* (Niles, Michigan: Arthur S. DeMoss Foundation, 1986), 59.

20. Ibid., 60.

21. Charles G. Finney, *Lectures on Revival of Religion* (New York: Fleming H. Revell, 1988), 22-34.

22. "Ministry Report" (Wheaton, Illinois: Concerts of Prayer International, 1992), 2.

23. Mike MacIntosh, letter, 23 March 1994, 2.

24. Sri Prabhakar, telephone conversation, 20 January 1994.

25. Joe Aldrich, telephone conversation, 8 February 1994.

When Broken Humble People Come Together

The room was filled with approximately one hundred pastors from every major denomination and independent group throughout the Pacific Northwest. They had gathered for training before a Billy Graham Evangelistic Crusade.

I stood before the group that morning and began my talk with a question.

"How many of you in this room are praying for revival, for spiritual awakening in your area of North America, for an extraordinary movement of God's Spirit to sweep through your church?"

No more than six or seven people raised their hands.

"How many of you are praying on a consistent basis? How many of you, when you look at your church and look at our nation, are seeing signs of revival—brokenness, confession and prayer that could only come from God?"

Practically no hands went up.

That was May 1983. For the next several years, I found this "no hands" response the same in the United States and around the world. If people were praying for revival, they weren't talking about it or admitting it, at least to me.

Eight years later in February 1991, I stood before a similar group of church leaders in the same city, preparing for another Billy Graham Crusade. "For the past twenty years, as an organizer of evangelistic crusades, I've visited with church and lay leaders in almost every region of the country," I said. "Everywhere I've gone I've asked people a question, the same one I'd like to ask you:

"How many of you here this morning are praying for revival, a spiritual awakening in our nation?"

Out of approximately 150 pastors and church leaders, more than 60 percent raised their hands.

I wasn't surprised. Since 1987, dozens of other Christian audiences to whom I had spoken around the country had begun raising their hands to acknowledge the reality of prayer for revival in the United States. Not only were many praying for an extraordinary spiritual awakening in their country, some were already seeing it unfold.

What these people have witnessed and what I have seen and examined—and in some cases participated in directly—is what I want to describe to you in this chapter.

A Pinprick of Light

The stories of God's renewal I'm about to relate represent just the beginning of an era in our nation's spiritual formation that's still being written.

Like past movements, the present, emerging awakening resists definition—yet it's real.

Like a pinprick of light in an ever-darkening national mood, God's small yet brilliant presence has pierced through unexpectedly. Many have yet to see it. Their "cave," their life, has been so dark for so long that they've forgotten what light looks like. These people have grown so accustomed to a daily world obscured by shootings, moral decay and personal despair that they can't see God in their midst. It's as if years of wandering without spiritual guidance and the conscious-yet-unwise choice to "explore new directions" have caused our nation to stumble into a dark and dangerous mine shaft. So many have wandered so far for so long, they've stopped looking for— even hoping for—light.

But others have seen it. They've caught God in the act of illuminating our world. Or to say it more accurately, He's caught them with their spiritual eyes wide open. You and I have the privilege of hearing their stories and celebrating what they've seen. As you meet these people, you will notice there is nothing outwardly extraordinary about them. In fact, as you see what remarkable things they've witnessed and are eager to talk about, as you share their stories with others, their names will fade from your memory. And that will leave you mulling over one question: "What in the world is God doing?"

This is the voice of spiritual awakening. This is what happens when broken, humbled people come together....

Ignition in Philadelphia

For years Paul Chaya had known Philadelphia to be a city of pride. He had grown up north of Philadelphia in Allentown, a mid-sized city known for its steel production. In that rough-and-tough city he had taught physical education for thirteen years at the Central YMCA. In 1981 Paul exercised an option to pursue theological training and graduated with a divinity degree. The pride he sensed often characterized and fueled political and racial conflicts. As he began to work more closely with the church and as he became senior pastor of a Baptist church in the Olney district, Paul saw that pride in its true colors—racism.

Though the story never made the front page of the *Philadelphia Inquirer*, the city reached a historic milestone in 1992—three thousand miles to the west of the "City of Brotherly Love." Paul remembers what happened.

"The turning point had come in January 1992. Two months earlier, Joe Aldrich came to Philadelphia to lead a seminar on prayer for the upcoming Greater Philadelphia Billy Graham Crusade scheduled for that June. The stories he told were almost unbelievable—stories of prayer, stories of people hungering for God, stories of pastors and laymen and women coming to the Lord as broken people.

"None of the church leaders in the room had heard anything like this, but we wanted it. We knew we weren't united as pastors. Here we were planning an evangelistic crusade to reach others with the Gospel in the Lord's name, and we couldn't find a common love for each other."[1]

Then the unexpected happened. Two months later, with the help of the Philadelphia Billy Graham Crusade Director Rick Marshall, Paul Chaya found himself on a plane with seven other fellow pastors bound for Portland and a retreat center on the picturesque Oregon coast.

"It was the first time I'd ever flown in a jet," said Paul. The retreat also marked another, more significant, first. On the first night, with all the men seated together for worship in the upper room of the Cannon Beach Conference Center, Paul came before the group of 160 pastors from Portland and his fellow ministers from Philadelphia. In a move unexpected by everyone present—including his five African-American, one Hispanic and one Anglo counterparts—Paul stood up, fully aware of Philadelphia's pride (and of his own), and made a painful confession.

"I need to say something to you all, something I've been thinking and praying about. It's something I can no longer keep to myself. *All my life I've been a racist.* I've just never wanted to admit it. As I look at you, my brothers from Philadelphia, I can't hide my sin. I need to ask your forgiveness. I need that tonight. I can't continue any longer under a false pretense and work for the Kingdom of God."

Before Paul had a chance to sit down, he was met by an African-American pastor whom he had come to know on the plane ride to Portland. Moments after the words of racial prejudice were out of Paul's mouth, the big man wrapped his arms around him and said, "You are forgiven." Then, speaking on behalf of the other African-Americans both in the room and beyond, the pastor said, "We need to ask your forgiveness, too. It [racial prejudice] happens on both sides." As the two men hugged, men throughout the room began embracing one another and thanking God for what was taking place.

"When I spoke up and told them what was in my heart, I didn't think about forgiveness, about what these men might do or say," said Paul. "Their response sat me down. They had so much reason to be upset. How could these men, these fellow-pastors, these brothers, have so much love for me? Had they led out and confessed the same thing to me, I might have retaliated. But they didn't. They responded by forgiving me and loving me.

"At that moment I was in the presence of God. Seeing my sin, a deep sense of humility came over me that caused me to look at my own attitudes and ask, 'How could I live this way for so much of my life?' The Holy Spirit convicted me. I was so broken, so thankful. That night I experienced the love of Christ that transcends woundedness and hurt."

Though the pastors ended their prayer summit on Thursday, they hadn't yet reached the peak. That night the group from Philadelphia met in a room at the Red Lion Inn in Portland. "We had just wanted to get together to discuss how to bring the prayer summit to Philadelphia," recalls Paul. "As we were talking and sharing, the Holy Spirit came upon us. At first I felt paralyzed. People couldn't kneel or stand. Words can't explain it, but the men in the room were overcome with tears. Some laid down on the floor, face down. Others laid down on beds, weeping and praying.

"One man cried, 'Lord, forgive us, make us what you

want us to be.' Like water coming up from a deep well, his words started a stream of remorse. It was like none of us could hold it in. Then, this deep, deep sorrow carried us back to God.

"'Give us the city, Lord! Give us the city!' cried another man. Again, one man's words spoke from the heart of every man in the room.

"'Make a great work through us and with us, Lord,' said another."

For nearly an hour, the group of pastors from Philadelphia cried out to God. Some continued to cry. Others prayed in silence.

"Then, slowly but clearly, the Holy Spirit ascended," Paul continued. "The crying and the words stopped. As each of us looked around the room, we realized that we had become one. Five African-Americans, one Hispanic and two whites had become one in Christ through God's Holy Spirit."

The group had traveled to Portland against stiff westerlies. They now went back to Philadelphia riding the wind of the Holy Spirit.

When Paul Chaya and his fellow pastors returned to Philadelphia and the pre-Crusade meetings, the people around them could see that something had happened. The pastors began praying that the reconciliation they had experienced would come to their fellow ministers. Four months later in May, for four days from Monday through Friday, 105 pastors gathered at the Harvey Cedars Conference Center on the New Jersey coast and sought God for unity.

The timing could not have been more ominous. A few

nights before, flames had licked the night skies as the Los Angeles riots left thirty-seven dead and more than fifteen hundred wounded. As the pastors scrunched together in the pews, one African-American pastor burned inside.

"I must tell all of you here, that I'm so angry about what's happening in L.A., I don't know if I can take communion."

A white pastor sitting nearby came over to the man and asked for forgiveness. Then a Hispanic pastor did the same. Something had been lit.

A Chinese pastor stood up. His voice was subdued.

"I must tell you that Asian people have often had bad feelings toward our black Christian brothers. But I must speak for myself.

"I would never think of saying the 'N' word, but down in my heart I wanted to. I thought it. I didn't know how to stop it. Tonight my heart is broken. I can't hide behind my collar of pious platitudes, because deep down I'm a racist. On the surface, I've looked pretty good, but deep down I'm filled with stereotypes of people like you in this room whose skin is a different color than mine."

"Years of bottled-up mistrust and hatred were poured out for the first time," said Paul. "There was such a sense of release. People confessed their sins to each other. The people they had despised listened and then forgave them. This was beyond human compassion. This could only be the Holy Spirit convicting people in an unusually powerful way."

On a riotous night of explosive hatred burning on the distant Pacific shore, a spark of pure light pierced years of racial darkness in Philadelphia. And the holy fire grew.

As Paul describes it, "Before November and Joe Aldrich's seminar, the attitude of many of us from Philadelphia working on the Crusade was, 'Let's put it together, let's do this program.' After the Pastors' Prayer Summit in May, the desire of everyone was, 'Let's meet Jesus.' "

And a city did. In the two years since the Billy Graham Crusade, four more Pastors' Prayer Summits in Philadelphia have touched the lives of 175 pastors.

Confessions and forgiveness have nurtured an ongoing sense of humility. As Paul says, "No one who has been to one of the summits sees color anymore, because everybody knows we've been saved by the grace of Jesus; He's the focal point."

Out of prayer and reconciliation has come a greater heart for evangelism. According to Paul Chaya, one youth pastor in Philadelphia, Mike McPherson, invited high school students from the city's public schools to attend a meeting designed "for anyone who wanted to get off drugs in twenty-four hours." Students from eighteen area schools came and listened to an evangelist share how a relationship with God through Jesus Christ offered the only true and permanent solution to all forms of addiction. By the end of the evening, twelve hundred had committed their lives to Christ.[2]

In the dark cave of drugs, these young people saw a pinprick of light, followed it, and found the Lord. The Holy Spirit had pierced through a youth climate of peer pressure and cynicism.

Look what had happened. What began as a private confession on the Oregon coast rippled through the city in an unanticipated and unplanned manner. Suddenly,

Charles Finney's words came to life again; revival is coming "when the ministers and laity are willing for God to promote spiritual awakening by whatever instrument He pleases."[3]

. . . And The Light Is Becoming Brighter

The prayer, reconciliation and evangelism ignited and sustained by the Holy Spirit in Philadelphia is just one expression of the Holy Spirit's unfolding work now going on in our nation.

What has become one of the most remarkable youth movements in the early 1990s came to life in a Southern Baptist Church in Nashville, Tennessee. One day, two high school girls went to their church youth pastor disillusioned that they were the only virgins they knew. Their concerns ultimately motivated leaders of the Southern Baptist Sunday School Board to produce a set of resources to help parents and their children understand that the Bible teaches sexual abstinence before marriage.

Were teenage youth willing to turn their backs on the fast-and-loose permissiveness around them? Were they willing to pledge themselves to abstinence based on a clearly biblical rationale? Yes! The concerns of two girls became the catalyst for thousands of young men and women across the nation to save sexual activity for marriage. The appropriate name of the cause became "True Love Waits."

As of December 1994 the ministry had encouraged nearly a quarter of a million teenage youth to make personal commitments of sexual abstinence before marriage. Sara Hughes was one of thirty high school students in her youth group at First Baptist Church in Richland, Washington, who were recognized in a recent Sunday worship service for making the following True Love Waits pledge:

> Believing that true love waits, I make a
> commitment to God, myself, my family, my friends,
> my future mate, and my future children
> to be sexually abstinent from this day until the day
> I enter into a biblical marriage relationship.

"I want my wedding night to be special," she says. "The one gift I have to give to my husband is my sexuality, and that's one gift I can't give to anyone else. The world doesn't understand that."[4]

And how! According to Sara, 75 percent of sophomores surveyed at her high school—three out of every four—believed there was nothing wrong with having sex before marriage.[5]

When has American society seen such a rising tide of teenage youth, like Sara, embrace such a clearly biblical position about sex that stems from a heart-felt commitment to God? Who could have awakened so many, in such a short time, to such a culturally unpopular stance? Who—but God?

Some would discount decisions like Sara's simply as a rebellious, counterculture statement in a promiscuous age. As a counselor in the Fairfax (Virginia) County Schools said, "Whatever is in vogue, you rebel the other way."[6] But listen to Paul Turner with The Baptist Sunday School Board, an agency of the Southern Baptist Convention responsible for nurturing True Love Waits into a movement endorsed by twenty-seven U.S. denominations and parachurch organizations (as well as groups in Canada and central Africa): "The pendulum has swung so far to the left in the secular revolution, teens have said this is enough. There's been a clear return to God by the young people in our country."[7]

The Promise of Promise Keepers

Our nation's youth are not the only ones experiencing a spiritual renaissance. In 1990, Bill McCartney, then head football coach at Colorado University, founded Promise Keepers as a "Christ-centered ministry dedicated to uniting men through vital relationships to become godly influences in their world."

The ministry clearly addressed a long-overdue need in our country:

> Wives, children, churches and communities all seem to agree that what we need today are men who are promise keepers: men who will not compromise the truth, men who are true to their word, men who are trustworthy. Promise Keepers is committed to igniting, equipping and uniting men to do just that—keep their promises. We base this objective in the promise-keeping nature of God. Because He is faithful to fulfill all of His promises, He is our model.[8]

In its first four years, Promise Keepers has reached thousands of men who are searching and longing for something more than what secular culture says is right and good. Maybe because their brokenness is so real, maybe because so many are now willing to turn to God, maybe because men have found a supportive vehicle for seeking the Lord together as Christian brothers—maybe for all these reasons and more—a phenomenon like Promise Keepers has flourished.

Threads in a Spiritual Fabric

Radical reconciliation among pastors in Philadelphia. A phenomenal return to sexual purity by America's youth. And a growing movement of men confessing that they've not been the husbands and fathers God has called them to be.

Are these merely three sporadic, unrelated happenings? Or are they three distinct threads in the fabric of a current spiritual phenomenon? As eye-opening and God-honoring as these stories are, they are just a glimpse of the tapestry God is now weaving. Every recent testimony, every story, every headline that resonates with the biblical model of Hezekiah and rings true with Finney's seven indicators—every undeniable truth that says "God is reviving His people, His church in an extraordinary way"—is bittersweet news. Each time I see evidence of revival I am both gleeful and concerned, almost in the same breath. Here's why.

On the one hand I am filled with awe at the power and presence of God in our midst. How can you not be amazed and thankful at seeing the Holy Spirit break the grip of prejudice, sexual temptation, church disunity and outright disinterest in God in people whose lives are genuinely reborn? Frankly, the life-changing experiences have so caused me to praise God that revival is upon us that I've unconsciously said to myself, "This is what revival looks like. This is what we can look for in the days and months to come." Revival is both a cause for celebration and a precursor to explosive evangelism.

The very real glee felt by an increasing number of Christians in our land is that "Revival is for real." So what's the problem? Just this: *In seeing the first signs of spiritual awakening, we think we've "seen it all."*

In our rush to identify and confirm what's happening nationwide, there's the temptation to say, "This *must* be revival, because it matches a similar movement in our nation's past." Human nature wants to label, organize, package and distribute spiritual truth. Even this book is an attempt to provide human handles so we can hold on to a spiritual reality that is so much greater and more wonderful than mere words can explain or describe. Yet by measuring what's happening today with what's happened in our nation's past, we can miss the point of revival in our day. In trying to define and understand the *what*, we miss out on the joy of appreciating the *Who*, God Himself. If the stories at the beginning of this chapter and throughout this book cause you to say, "Wow, that's incredible. . . ." I hope I've caught you in mid-sentence, because if you look at what's really happening, the only possible conclusion you can make is that God is reviving His people in our time. And what He most wants is for them to know Him personally.

God at the Center

The best way, the *only* way, to understand the current movement and appreciate what it can mean in your life is to realize that the ongoing phenomenon we call spiritual awakening is centered completely and totally in God. The things happening in our country—which are unique from any past spiritual awaking in United States history—confirm God's nature and purposes laid out in His revealed Word. There are at least three reasons why I believe this is so.

If you've read any of the prophetic doomsday books of the 1970s and '80s, you might be surprised we're still around. If you can't recall the titles, maybe you'll recall the gist of the message, which was "things will get worse before they get better." Generally speaking, the authors based their working theology on a carefully constructed scenario of selected Scriptures and economic/geo-political warning signs. Because some of their arguments seemed so convincing at the time, two things occurred. The first (and obvious) result was that many Christians braced themselves for inevitable national or global catastrophe.

A second, more subtle result went unnoticed: if God's purpose ultimately leads us to Armageddon, then Christians cannot expect any national spiritual reawakening to occur. Indeed, the thinking went, as long as our country remained on a course of ungodly behavior with people turning their backs on the Christian faith, then God's judgment—*not* spiritual awakening—could be the only outcome.

So what has happened in the past several years? More and more throughout our land, we're seeing the dual presence of darkness and light. Like the cave that I wandered into as a teenager, the destructive forces in our world seem overpowering and ready to swallow us up. But the truth is that God's light has never been put out.

In some of the smallest, most unsuspecting corners of our nation, the light of God's truth has shined through. Two things have happened: not only have people seen the depth of the darkness in which they've been living, but more importantly, they've been astounded and drawn to the light. To make one more critical step in the analogy: the light of revival is not a candle that Christians are able to kindle by rubbing human will and desire together, nor is revival's light the creation of worried believers who can't find their way. Rather, it is the new emergence of the God who was there all along. Revival springs from God's initiation, not from our determination. Revival is the new light and life of God that comes in His time for His purposes, to lead us out of wandering and back to Himself—if His people finally have the spiritual eyes to see.

While Sara Hughes' pledge of sexually purity is the promise of True Love Waits, the strength to carry out such a promise comes only from God—the God who is now awakening her and thousands like her to Himself. The forgiveness and reconciliation Paul Chaya experienced came through a Pastors' Prayer Summit, but the freedom from prejudice and guilt he knows today continues because the Holy Spirit is alive and well, not because some human ministry is effective.

Why are broken, humbled people coming together to find healing and wholeness in God? The first thing to understand is that *the world's darkness and God's truth and light are both present at the same time.* To people like Sara

Hughes and Paul Chaya, the world's present darkness isn't necessarily a prelude to Armageddon, but the backdrop against which God's pinprick of light can be clearly seen. The fact is their stories are not isolated happenings. Because many people have been drawn to the same light, a second key understanding of the current revival must be considered.

When God Works through a Person

Pick up a leading news magazine or read through the national news section of your daily paper and you're bound to read about one or more Christian organizations making headlines:

"Making a Pledge: Promise Keepers calls, and men answer with vows to reclaim role of 'godly' leadership"[9]

"Students 'taking stand' for prayer in schools"[10]

" 'True Love Waits' for Some Teen-Agers"[11]

The accompanying stories make it obvious that each of these efforts is highly organized. The followers are so united in their cause that they seem to be on a campaign. But what the stories may not reveal is that each of these Christian causes is an expression of faith that has grown out of the heart of a person.

Pastors' Prayer Summits didn't begin with a formal declaration and by-laws. They grew out of a pastors' prayer breakfast that Joe Aldrich led in Salem, Oregon, back in the fall of 1988. In the middle of his presentation he asked the leaders, "What would it take to attract the blessing of God among your community?"[12] "Dr. Joe" had already found a prerequisite for God's blessing a community in Psalm 133: "How good and pleasant it is when brothers live together in unity" (v.1). The pastors saw the connection and that morning eagerly agreed to attend a weekend retreat. Their meeting the next February marked the first Pastors' Prayer Summit. By the end of 1994, nearly 250 similar gatherings had been held.

When Dr. Joe spoke to a room of tired church leaders in Salem, Oregon, one morning in the late 1980s, he never imagined he was really speaking to the hurts and wounds of pastors throughout the nation who didn't know how to make a new beginning with God.

Through Christians such as Joe Aldrich, Bill McCartney and others, it's clear that God brings about revival through the heart of people who, like Hezekiah, are "doing what was good and right and faithful before the LORD his God" (2 Chronicles 31:29).

The second key to understanding revival in our time is that *through the hearts of broken individuals, God can reach an entire nation.* By speaking through the brokenness of one person, God gives us a living illustration of how He can forgive, change and empower a church, a city-wide gathering, even an entire nation.

In noting individuals like Bill McCartney, Joe Aldrich, Bill Bright and Billy Graham—people whom I consider to be at the forefront of today's revival stirrings—I have not referred to them as "leaders." There's a reason for this. From Hezekiah on down, revival has not depended upon the "leadership ability" of a particular person.

- George Whitefield preached with passion and theatrical flair, yet the First Great Awakening did not rest on his sermons.

- Jeremiah Lanphier was a faithful pray-er and promoter able to draw people to his noon-day New York City prayer meetings, yet he was not the main reason thousands eventually came to Christ.

In none of these instances did God allow any person or group to take credit for the extraordinary work and results of His Holy Spirit. I believe anyone whom God is using to further today's spiritual awakening understands this.

Rather than claiming an exclusive truth through sharp directives, such facilitators embody the truth through the example of their lives. Therefore, rather than feeling the need to control, shape and mold what they see as their ministry, they accurately see that "their" ministry really belongs to God. They realize their biggest challenge as "leaders" is to resist the desire to blow on the flame of their vision for fear it may go out. Instead, their calling is to get out of the way and let God be the keeper of the light.

If you look at the people who embody the early stirrings of revival in America, you will come to another conclusion: no one person is (or will be) behind this spiritual phenomenon. Some may enjoy more than their share of headlines, yet they themselves would be the first to admit that God alone is the One who deserves the publicity and the credit for true spiritual transformation, a spiritual change that's beyond human understanding or control.

To repeat: what we're seeing in the infant stages of

revival is a miracle of God, not a creation of people. For all of their attraction, the testimonies of spiritual awakening do not contain the whole truth. When we watch a roomful of pastors crying, their pride and egos broken in two, it is tempting to say, "That's revival going on." Well . . . yes . . . and not quite.

It's critical to keep in mind that the expressions of today's movement—emotional outpouring, prayers of confession and repentance, even while they are God-breathed—are not total, accurate definitions of revival itself. They are only the human means of expressing something much deeper inside a radically changed heart. The amazing outpouring of people now being made new again in Christ is both a great temptation and an opportunity. The *temptation* is getting so caught up in a movement that we miss the *opportunity* of falling so in love with God that nothing else matters.

It's impossible to overemphasize the fact that the sole focus of any revival is God alone and that its sole purpose is to honor Him. For years, I've searched for a way to grasp and convey this truth. Whenever I've tried to explain it, I've ended up preaching more than teaching.

One day I spoke to a small group of church leaders who began the meeting by voicing their doubts that spiritual awakening was even possible in our time. Since I didn't know these men and women (and they surely didn't know me), I decided to put their skepticisms to the side and tell them a little bit about who I was. That's when I found my illustration for revival. The analogy I had been seeking for years was part of my own story.

A Land Ripe for Revival

I grew up on a farm in northeastern Mississippi home-steaded by my grandfather, Joseph Whitefield Phillips. This Primitive Baptist circuit rider with a revivalist middle name had built a large home out of sandstone rocks. It was perched on a bluff and looked out on rolling fields where cotton, soybeans and corn grew. As a small boy, I could stand on the front porch and watch as combines and tractors crawled through the scorching heat, my uncles and cousins at the wheel. I could always tell by the looks on their faces and by the conversation over dinner if it had been a good harvest. But I never understood the full meaning of what was at stake in the autumn months that followed. When the days grew shorter and darker, I came to see the meaning of the harvest.

Every fall it happened. After the cotton, corn and soybeans were picked, the stalks and the left-over vegetation would be turned under. The dry soil that summer had turned into hard clods was dissolved by tractor disks. When the breaking was complete, the earth became finer than corn meal. Fertilizing occurred in the early spring, then planting in April or May.

In the late spring I could see my Uncle Millard standing in a sea of dark brown earth that held our family's future. Against an orange sky at dusk, his weather-beaten body made a striking silhouette. I would see him stoop over, pick up a handful of moist, cool soil, and let it run through his hands. Then he would look up, and I knew what he was saying, "God, we've done all that we can do, and now this crop is in your hands. The ground is tilled. The fertilizer is there. The seeds are in the ground. We can't touch them until they grow. Only with the rain and sun You bring will we see new life."

This picture captures my own living analogy for the time of spiritual awakening that awaits our nation. For years, our country, our land, has produced a bountiful spiritual harvest through believers who, like sprouting seeds, have lived the normal Christian life; they have fulfilled their purpose and died so that new life could grow. In extraordinary seasons of awakening, when humble people have admitted to God, "We've done all that we can do," the Lord has seen fit to rain down His Holy Spirit. The "harvests" that people such as George Whitefield, Jeremiah Lanphier and Charles Finney participated in revived a dead land not permanently, but for a season of years.

From most outward appearances today, many would doubt that another extraordinary spiritual harvest could come from the land we call home. There are too many weeds. There has been too much drought. And there's a desperate shortage of caring workers. Yet even these things cannot deny a fact that is now coming to the surface: America is experiencing two distinct "harvests."

One is a harvest of seed that has never known the ground of truth. Without the right and natural place in which to grow, without the surrounding "nutrients" of Scripture, these seeds, these people, have sprouted unsatisfying roots that have nowhere to go. America is filled with such seeds—people who sink their roots into dark places where soil and sunlight are nonexistent. Instead of maturing into the creation God intended, they grow according to their unrooted condition. Instead of soil, they seek unhealthy substitutes—destructive chemicals (alcohol and drugs), unnatural, destructive influences (promiscuity, homosexuality) and the wrong balance of God-given elements (money, people and possessions). Seeds allowed to rot prove the truth of The Agronomist's Law: "No root, no shoot, no fruit."

This ungodly crop of America is the harvest of a people who have never known God's true ground of the Holy Spirit, the Bible and the Church. They will never grow to be all that God truly intended unless they discover a true, growing environment where America's other harvest is silently waiting to bloom.

Except one element is missing.

For at least the past half-century, our nation has been suffering a spiritual drought. Ever since the end of World War II, our churches, our schools and our families have often failed to sink their roots into healthy soil. Over time, the guiding truth of God's Word has lost ground to individually minded values. As self-centered desires have eroded God-centered principles and relationships, our people have grown up less and less fulfilled. And in the mean time, something else has happened. The land has become arid.

For whatever reason, over the last twenty or thirty years the rain of the Holy Spirit has been increasingly absent across our land. Many Christians have felt this drought; many churches have experienced it. Yet the fact is, many "good seeds" have found a home in the healthy, growing ground of Christ-centered churches, small groups and one-to-one relationships. These pockets of believers remind me of how soybean seeds can exist for months in soil without rain. These are the people who are ready for the Holy Spirit to rain down, the people ready to come alive—the people ripe for revival.

In one way, the seed that's rotting away and the seed that's ready to awaken from the ground are strangely alike; each can go no further and grow no further without outside help. In the context of today's revival stirrings, you and I are like the farmer who admits, "I've done all that I possibly can, Lord. Now, You must bring the rain."

And look what is already happening! Sprinkled across our nation, God's early rains have begun to fall. On our youth. On men. On pastors who know what true brokenness, confession and repentance are all about—and who know God is doing something extraordinary in them and through them.

In specific areas of our country, on specific groups of broken, humbled people, God's Holy Spirit is beginning to lightly rain. Previous revivals have known this same, refreshing Spirit. Yet what's happening today is unique from anything our country has ever experienced, and uniquely personal to every life He's touching:

- The pastor who can't speak through his tears.
- The high school sophomore who can't resist the temptation of the moment, and who yet can't forget the daily promise he or she has made to God.
- The business executive who wants to get in touch with his emotions and his God—who finds a way to do so with other committed promise keepers.

What unites these individuals is the God now bringing His people together—on their knees. For them, and for you, true spiritual awakening rests with one action. And because revival comes in God's own time, this one action is all we can actually do. What the Bible teaches, what Charles Finney suggests and what Christians you've read about are committed to is the one element that will bring us face-to-face with God. That one element, the key to our nation's revival, our own personal revival, is prayer.

Endnotes

1. Paul Chaya, telephone conversation, 18 October 1994.

2. Ibid.

3. Charles G. Finney, *Lectures on Revival of Religion* (New York: Fleming H. Revell, 1988), 33.

4. Sara Hughes, telephone conversation, 22 November 1994.

5. Ibid.

6. "Virginity is New Counterculture Among Area Teens," *Washington Post*, 21 November 1993, sec. A, 27.

7. Paul Turner, telephone conversation, 8 November 1994.

8. "What is a Promise Keeper", promotional brochure (Colorado Springs: Promise Keepers, 1994).

9. *The Herald* (Everett, Washington), 1 October 1994, E1.

10. Tony Mauro, *USA Today*, 15 September 1993, 4A.

11 "'True Love Waits' for Some Teenagers," *The New York Times*, 21 June 1993.

12. Joe Aldrich, telephone conversation, 8 February 1994.

CHAPTER FIVE

Why Prayer Is the Key

Several years ago something began to shake up my daily routine. At first, I was startled. The news made me more and more excited. I sat up in my chair, delighted and encouraged by what I was hearing.

In the spring of 1989, Sterling Huston, Director of North American Ministries for the Billy Graham Evangelistic Association, invited me to join another Crusade director, Larry Turner, at the Red Carpet Lounge at the Seattle-Tacoma International Airport. We were meeting to discuss how we might pray for an upcoming Crusade in Portland, Oregon. The key person joining us that afternoon was Dr. Joe Aldrich. Within minutes "Dr. Joe," as he's commonly known, presented us with a remarkable vision of how concerted, organized prayer could unify a city and build the greatest Crusade possible. This wasn't a typical, monthly gathering of fifty or sixty people. Joe could see hundreds, perhaps thousands of people coming together to pray for Portland, a city whose church leaders had been mistrustful of each other over the past thirty years.

Joe made it clear that this vision would take two years to unfold. Since most Crusades work on a one-year cycle, we didn't see how it could be accomplished. Still, this was the first time someone had laid out such an ambitious, heart-felt desire for long-term prayer prior to a Crusade. Unknown to us at the time, the Portland Crusade would happen three years later but already new winds of revival were stirring in the Northwest. Historically, prayer-stirred revival had always led to large numbers of people coming to Christ. At the time, no one could predict that Joe's vision would become greater than even he envisioned. None of us in that room had any idea that concerted prayer for Portland would be God's catalyst for evangelism as thousands came to Christ at five Crusade meetings at the city's Civic Stadium.

A "Black-and-White" Answer to Prayer

Even before the Portland Crusade I would experience revival stirrings of another sort. In January 1991 I was directing the Washington State Billy Graham Crusade in the Seattle-Tacoma area. The logistical challenges were unprecedented and enormous. We had only four months lead-time, just one-third of the time needed to plan most crusades. This was a unique crusade in Mr. Graham's ministry in that it would be held back-to-back in two major indoor, domed stadiums, the Tacoma Dome and the Kingdome in Seattle. But there was another "first," one of great, spiritual significance, that shed new light on the need for prayer to *further the spiritual awakening God is bringing about in our day.*

Early in the Crusade's planning stages, several prayer intercessors in the Seattle-Tacoma area said they especially wanted to move into the stadium sites to fast and pray for the crusade's evangelistic meetings. They wanted to pray for the four evangelistic meetings at the Tacoma Dome and the Kingdome as the events took place. To my knowledge, it was the first time in forty years of Billy Graham Crusade meetings that local residents had volunteered to actually live in the Crusade's stadia, from the time the site was first arranged, to fast and pray in an organized effort.

Naturally, I was totally supportive. As many as eighty people began to fast and pray one to two hours a day, some during free time at their jobs, others at home. Some people prayed as many as eight hours a day. These dedicated pray-ers said, "We want to pray at the stadia, we want to pray for the stadium, the workers and all the people who will be part of the meetings." Though the stadium officials told us there were laws against anyone residing on the premises, they agreed to let Crusade volunteers use two rooms. I suspected these stadium officials perceived the Crusade as just another event. Yet I sensed they saw the value of prayer. I sensed they knew that they and their fellow workers needed prayer. So, they graciously agreed to allow Crusade volunteers come and pray for the several days they had requested.

The first major gathering was held on Thursday night,

April 3, at the Tacoma Dome. The stadium was packed to capacity even though the Seattle-Tacoma region received a record rainfall. The deluge that flooded the freeways caused Mr. Graham to say, somewhat tongue-in-cheek, "I thought I should preach on Noah's ark!" In a room beneath the bleachers, a group of more than eighty men and women gathered to intercede in prayer and ask God's protection and direction for the meeting. During the prayer time one person spoke up.

"As I've been praying, I'm seeing black and white figures. Not that some are black and others are white. These figures are both black and white. They're evil. We need to pray against them." No one in the room could understand what this was about, yet the group began to pray against these unknown images.

Three days later on Sunday afternoon, I was confirming last-minute details at the Kingdome for the final evangelistic meeting of the Crusade. The chief security officer found me and said, "We've got a problem. Some gay activists are out in front of the stadium, passing out condoms." The official explained that since the protest conflicted with our purposes, and since we had rented the facility, he had authority to ask them to leave.

"There's another problem, though," he said. "They want to come inside the Kingdome."

"As a matter of security, what do you think about that?" I asked him.

"Well," he said, "if they come in, they'll have to take off their habits. You see, they're dressed like nuns. They're all in black and white."

God had already shown the intercessors to pray against

an organized onslaught that we couldn't see, but that He knew was coming!

"Something" Called Prayer

Something was happening, something I didn't fully understand—something that would prepare me for a growing spiritual awakening I already believed was beginning in America. This "something" was prayer. It was more than how God had faithfully answered someone's request to intervene. It was more than testimony, more than praise. All my life I had heard stories, I had seen, I had believed that God worked through prayer to mend broken relationships, heal emotional and physical wounds, make "the impossible" real for His glory. But this was different. By the early 1990s, as I traveled to different cities throughout the United States, I felt and wondered if something historic was taking place.

As I talked to church leaders and lay persons, as I listened and observed, meditated and prayed, I kept coming back to Charles Finney, the great revivalist of the nineteenth century. Though 130 years old, Finney's "Seven Indicators for Spiritual Awakening" were fresh in my mind. As you recall from chapter three, Finney believed revival would come:

1. When the sovereignty of God indicates that revival is near.
2. When wickedness grieves and humbles Christians.
3. When there is a spirit of prayer for revival.
4. When the attention of ministers is directed toward revival and spiritual awakening.

5. When Christians confess their sins one to another.

6. When Christians are willing to make the sacrifices necessary to carry out the new movement of God's Spirit.

7. When the ministers and laity are willing for God to promote spiritual awakening by whatever instrument he pleases.[1]

Prayer: the Heartbeat of God

By the early 1990s, Finney's indicators were becoming more and more relevant to the declining American culture. The only indicator we had not seen in North America was number five, "When Christians confess their sins to one another." Yet that began to change. As the crusade in Seattle ended and as my attention shifted to the crusade in Portland, I began to hear about some unusual meetings, the Pastors' Prayer Summits, in which pastors had come together and openly confessed practically every sin known to man.

This in itself was eye-opening. I, for one, was on guard. So many times I had seen confession lead to gossip. Yet as I learned about these extraordinary times of confession, gossip was nowhere to be heard. There could be only one explanation: when the white-hot light of God's spirit of conviction fell on His people, when one person confessed his sin, all were convicted to whatever degree they were guilty. The result was that no one was excluded from conviction or confession, and cleansing came to everyone.

It should not have surprised me that the catalyst behind these meetings was Joe Aldrich.

Never before had all of Finney's seven indicators for

spiritual awakening come to fruition in our generation. I'll be the first to admit that the next Great Awakening can't be forecast or confirmed by one man's list of characteristics. I don't know if Finney was accurate in all that he said. I'm not convinced that each of his seven indicators needs to be operative. But if Finney was correct, then everything was in place for a major spiritual awakening in our time.

Hearing about the pastors' confessions was merely the beginning. *Since that time, based on conversations I've had with Christian leaders and lay persons, based on what I've read and what I know, God has been stirring Christians across our country to pray daily for spiritual awakening, for revival in our nation:*

- Never in our generation, perhaps not in our century, has such a need for prayer for revival been felt by Christians in this country *until now.*

- Never in this time has the voice of prayer for revival been so intense and on the rise *until now.*

- Never in this time has the scope of prayer for revival come from so many different and diverse denominations *until now.*

- Never in this time have the results of prayer for revival been so apparent *until now.*

- Never in this time has the growing hunger for

prayer been so strong for what God will do in our nation through revival *until now.*

Here are just a few of the many examples regarding this new movement of prayer:

- In Manhattan, Montana, Nell Barr, a homemaker and mother of three, is one of a dedicated group in her church who gathers in a room to pray for the Sunday worship service as it takes place. Several years ago this was not happening. "People always knew that prayer was part of the Christian life, but they never really acknowledged the power of prayer," says Nell. "Through prayer groups now meeting in the United States, I believe there's a turning back to God in this country. I believe there's a renewed understanding that God has made prayer an avenue to connect His church to the power of heaven."[2]

- In Bayshore, Long Island, Rev. Larry Mancini, a church pastor, received a phone call from a long-time personal friend in another state. "He called specifically to ask me if I would go with him to attend a prayer meeting at the Brooklyn Tabernacle," says Larry. Several weeks later, Larry and his wife, along with several pastoral colleagues and their spouses, drove into Brooklyn and attended an extraordinary evening service of singing, open prayer and confession. As he rode home that evening, Larry knew something very real, something of God, had been stirred inside him: "I need more in my life than what's presently happening, something I haven't seen before in my life," he admitted to his friends. "In fact, beyond my church I'm definitely seeing a hunger for a relationship with Christ through the Holy Spirit not defined through a systematic theology."[3]

- Through See You at the Pole, one million junior and senior high students around the country gathered in circles around the flag poles of their respective schools on September 21, 1994, to pray for God's presence, strength and direction in their classrooms, homes, cities and towns. Says Paul Fleischmann, Executive Director of the National Network for Youth Ministries (a ministry that spearheads the annual See You at the Pole event), "Five years ago, you could not have gotten this kind of response from prayer. I couldn't picture beach kids in Southern California, where I grew up, doing what we're seeing today. I was skeptical—and as wrong as I could be."[4]

And Fleischmann is certain that the movement is not humanly motivated. Recently, after announcing the event to members at a meeting of the National Press Club in Washington, D.C., a reporter said to him, "Come on, you guys aren't student-led. You've told them what to do." Fleischmann replied, "When was the last time you told a million teenagers to do something, and they did it?" The reporter said nothing.[5]

Perhaps you see such outbreaks of prayer becoming more and more common and think, *I celebrate the fact that more and more Christians are praying today. I just don't know if I would call it "revival." Coming to God as broken, humbled people who want to be alive in Christ seems like the normal Christian life.*

Exactly!

Revival—the extraordinary work of the Holy Spirit now alive in pockets of Americans through conviction, confession and repentance—is the most normal thing God could ever do in individuals' lives and in our nation. By normal I don't mean occasionally crediting God for an answered prayer or the thousands of daily assurances God gives His people through their regular quiet times. What's normal about revival is God's infinite desire and ability to turn the lives of individuals and churches upside-down so that their pride, indifference and disobedience spills out and is seen for what it is—sin. Through the resulting repentance the Holy Spirit is "bringing back to life that which was dead"—which is exactly what's happening right now across our nation through prayer. Such extraordinary prayer happenings, such as the ones you've just read about, lead us to a watershed in understanding today's revival stirrings:

While the biblical evidence of Hezekiah and others *shows that revival is of God;*

While historical precedence *suggests that revival in our nation could come again;*

While our ever-darkening world, now being pierced by extraordinary truth, *indicates that the early light of revival is already in our midst* . . .

While all these things make a strong case for spiritual awakening in our time, revival—the extraordinary means God uses to restore the normal Christian life—will flourish as we find God at work in our nation, and in you and me, *through prayer*.

Like revival itself, this extraordinary movement of prayer is now spreading across our nation in ways we don't even realize. When we look at prayer, we are seeing the heart of revival because prayer is the heartbeat of God. Without prayer, none of the confession and repentance we're seeing (and are still yet to see) could take place. When we look at today's revival stirrings, we will see why prayer is foundational to spiritual awakening.

Charles Finney noted that revival is simply normal Christianity. In a normal family relationship you expect clear communication between all the members. For the Christian, prayer is that clear line of communication in an intimate relationship with God. We see in the parable of the Prodigal Son specifically how prayer shows the early beginnings of revival. As the son returned home and reestablished his communication and relationship with the father, the father turned to the elder son and said, " . . . this brother of yours was dead and is alive again; he was lost and is found" (Luke 15:32). The Greek word for "alive again" is *anazaho*, which means "brought back to life." So, what the father really meant was that his son was now revived!

The Church is often slumbering and comatose and needs to be brought back to life. Today the Church is filled with prodigals who, even though they are Christian, are dead to the will of the Father and rebelling against the Father.

Why has this happened?

One of the main reasons is that we in the Church have become willing victims of a frantic culture that robs us of time. In 1980 we were told that, because of advances in technology, we would be working only an average of thirty-six hours a week instead of forty. Today, however, Americans are working an average of forty-nine hours a week, plus the commute to and from work! Exhausted Christians who want to be brought back to life are making the time to pray. They realize that without a clear and constant line of communication with God, they are spiritually disabled and emotionally bankrupt. Regardless of the cost, these individuals are ready to reach out to God, to come home and be brought back to life by a Father who's waiting with open arms.

Perhaps without knowing it, these Christians are experiencing the fact that prayer is always the greatest indicator of spiritual awakening. Why does God want us, as individuals, to pray so that He can corporately address the needs of His prodigal Church? It's beyond us. It's beyond human understanding why God would want our silent longings and muttered whispers. Yet, He does. And through our prayer, revival begins.

Prayer unleashes power.

Power is necessary for the revitalization of the church.

A revitalized church is a unified and Christ-focused church.

A unified and Christ-focused church is necessary for evangelism.

Evangelism is necessary for discipleship.

Discipleship is necessary for a maturing, reproducing church.

A maturing, reproducing church is necessary for the building of the Kingdom.

And the building of the Kingdom is necessary for the return of Christ.

Revitalization, evangelism, discipleship and building the Kingdom for His return—it all begins in prayer. Prayer that begins in the heart of God and moves to the heart of the individual, the Christian whose heart is turned toward God. When God raises up a person like Joe Aldrich, Bill McCartney or Bill Bright, all of whom bring like-minded prodigals together, then we see that prayer is foundational to revival. Prayer helps Christians become both concerned about their relationship with the Father and willing to reestablish communication with Him regardless of the sacrifice required.

The place of prayer, the need for prayer in the Christian life, has always been central. What's new is that over the past several years, Christians are now praying with an increasing earnestness and intensity that hasn't been seen in decades, perhaps generations. What makes the prayer movement in the United States and Canada so intriguing and noteworthy is that its presence and force are continuing to grow right now. By the time you read these words, the unique, corporate expressions of prayer will, perhaps, be even more prominent than I'm able to describe in these pages. All you need to do is meet humbled, broken Christians who describe how the God who's stirring our nation to revival has brought them to their knees. God is using prayer to awaken Christians throughout North America in four distinct ways. In the fabric of the current revival stirrings, these are just a few of the many brilliant and varied threads.

Jim Tharp and "The School of Prayer"

In 1975 I met Jim Tharp, who was then senior pastor at a church in Albuquerque, New Mexico. Over the years our friendship deepened. In 1986 our paths crossed again as I was in the midst of directing the "Peaks to Plains" Billy Graham Crusade, a five-state evangelistic outreach to Montana, North Dakota, South Dakota, Colorado and Wyoming. Right away I could tell there was something unusual about Jim. He told me he had recently met with some fellow pastors in a "pastoral institute" sponsored by his denomination. The focus of the conference had been prayer; one Christian man had completed forty days of prayer and fasting and told the group about it. Jim told me the man's testimony and the prayer he experienced over those days had gripped him. "Never before had I majored in prayer," he said, "but I began to discover something of the power of prayer as seen in the life of our Lord and the early church."[6]

The importance of prayer, the power of prayer, the need for prayer in his own life and in the church—it was all so powerful, Jim couldn't keep it to himself. Instead, he began to relate what he knew to others through an eight-hour seminar he called a "School of Prayer." In the school, Jim distinguished Great Awakenings (which he defines as "mighty movings of the Holy Spirit who falls on sinners in the land") from revivals ("the spiritual renewal of the Church itself").[7] In the school he also described spiritual warfare and how a Christian could establish a discipline of prayer and Bible study.

The School of Prayer seminars have received such great interest throughout the United States that Jim recently resigned his pastorate to invest more time in teaching on prayer. What's more significant than the thousands of people who've come to learn to pray in these sessions is what God has been doing through individuals and churches.

"When believers turn to God in meaningful prayer, they undergo an awakening," says Jim. "They start to see their undoneness, coldness, hardness, self-righteousness and whatever else that is displeasing to God. As they respond in brokenness and repentance, they are cleansed and renewed in the fullness of the Holy Spirit.[8]

"In a majority of churches, we've had reports of a new anointing of the Holy Spirit for humility, conviction, repentance, faith, obedience, witness and every Kingdom-advancing ministry. This is often called revival, and properly so."[9]

Since he began the schools, Jim says he's seen "a breaking down of prejudices, a melting of cold hearts, a destruction of suspicions, a letting go of petty differences, a new love, appreciation and understanding of fellow pastors/brothers and sisters regardless of their theological, philosophical or denominational backgrounds."[10]

The most convincing reality of prayer through Jim Tharp's school, as well as any other means of revival, is that God becomes real in ways people could never imagine. "For years I viewed prayer as just another part of being a Christian, like reading the Bible at dinner. The School of Prayer has revolutionized our prayer life," says Nell Barr, who grew into the daily discipline of praying one hour each morning with her husband. "At the end of the hour I don't leave the prayer time; Jesus just continues to walk with me."[11]

Nell remembers when Jim told the story of the renowned pastor Charles Spurgeon who, while giving people a tour of his church prior to his sermons, led them down into the basement. "Here, I want you to see the power plant of the church," he said. When Spurgeon opened the door, there was a roomful of men and women deep in prayer. After hearing the story, Nell Barr felt moved by the Holy Spirit to form a similar "power plant" of continuous pray-ers who would intercede during all eight hours of Tharp's annual School of Prayer session in Bozeman, Montana. As she says, "Every time we step into that prayer room, we step out of a realm of time and into a realm of communion."[12]

The proof that God is at work in our land awakening His people is that His followers such as Nell Barr and Jim Tharp are becoming changed people, sometimes against their own will. After all, if spiritual awakening means blessing, it also means sacrifice. Admits Jim, "I've given up an old schedule that made too much time for socializing, reading things that didn't count and wasting hours either watching television or working on matters of personal interest only. While I believe theology is an important subject, for instance, I no longer find it's my number one interest; prayer is first and foremost. I've given up my late evenings in order to retire for rest and sleep so that I might get up early and meet the Lord."[13]

The story of Jim Tharp is just one tremor in the stirrings now taking place throughout the country:

- In Fallon, Nevada, Reverend Duane Vaughn notes "a definite awareness of God's presence and involvement in people's lives that's not coming from me but from the Holy Spirit. You can just sense the presence of God in the sanctuary. And we're seeing a real bonding across age levels in ten people, from high school youth to seniors who've made the commitment to take one hour of quality time out of their day to pray."[14]

- In the Yakima valley of southeast Washington State, according to Nell Barr, pastors from various denominations are meeting weekly to pray together. When Nell asked one of the ministers, "Do you feel there is an undercurrent of revival in our nation?" he immediately said, "Yes."

- At a church in Davenport, Iowa, a group of five to twelve men meet early in the morning for an hour each weekday before work. Their sole reason for meeting is to pray for revival to come to their city and their nation.

If prayers for revival have been stirred through individuals and small groups, prayer as a part of today's spiritual awakening has also found a voice through corporate expressions. One of the most significant of these has brought praying Christians together by the thousands.

Concerts of Prayer

In 1988, David Bryant left InterVarsity Christian Fellowship to devote his complete time and effort to nurturing what he sensed was a grass-roots prayer movement. He founded Concerts of Prayer International (COPI) "to serve the Church by promoting, equipping and mobilizing movements of united prayer that seek God for spiritual awakening and worldwide evangelization."[15] The ministry's name was inspired by evangelist J. Edwin Orr who wrote in his book, *The Eager Feet*, "The Concert of Prayer for revival in the 1780s in Great Britain and in the 1790s in the United States, and the renewed Concert of Prayer in both countries . . . was clearly demonstrated to be the prime factor in motivating and equipping Christians for service in a worldwide movement which totally eclipsed the military might of the nations at the battle of Waterloo . . . . As in the first half of the century (the early 1800s), practically every missionary vision (from 1858 onward) was launched by men revived in the awakenings in the sending churches."[16]

As Bryant himself writes, "Historically speaking, the primary focus of Concerts has been on two major agendas: Christians prayed for Christ's *fullness* (Ephesians 1:22-23) to be revealed in His Church to empower them to accomplish the task that was before them. They also prayed for the *fulfillment* (Ephesians 1:10) of His saving purposes among the nations through an awakened, consecrated Church. The same twofold agenda prevails today.

"And so Concerts of Prayer helps describe Christians united on a regular basis to seek fullness and fulfillment. Extraordinary, united prayer is not determined so much by how long one prays or how often, but rather that Christians do pray, that they pray for those things most on God's heart, and that they do so together—'in concert.' "[17]

Practically speaking, Concerts of Prayer took the form of large, public meetings, usually in a church building. Typically, each concert followed a structured, two-hour format:

- Celebration (ten minutes)
- Preparation (twenty minutes)
- Dedication (five minutes)
- Seeking for Fullness/Awakening in the Church (thirty   minutes)
- Seeking for Fulfillment/Mission among the Nations (thirty minutes)
- Testimonies: What has God said to us here? (ten minutes)
- Grand Finale (fifteen minutes)

In 1990 I led a city-wide Concert of Prayer in Tacoma, Washington, using the format suggested by David. I certainly believed in the need to pray, the centrality of Scripture and the belief that God would use our time, as David suggests, to pray for Christ's fullness and His fulfillment of His saving purposes.

Who can argue that God has not used David Bryant to stir our nation to pray? In the first six years of this ministry, from 1988-1994, Bryant announced that COPI had conducted more than 350 city-wide Concerts of Prayer worldwide, led nearly half a million people in "intensive prayer events," and helped equip more than thirty thousand pastors and thousands more local church prayer leaders.

Concerts of Prayer has played an important part of the current, ongoing prayer movement in America. Through the vision and efforts of David Bryant and the ministry he's founded, many Christians, who perhaps wouldn't otherwise, have come together in prayer.

I believe the emergence of Concerts was part of God's perfect timing. Christians were used to coming to large gatherings, from Billy Graham Crusades to seminars held by Basic Youth Conflicts. So, when Concerts of Prayer began, two things happened. First, Christians were encouraged to gather *en masse*, in effect saying to themselves and each other, "I'm going to seek God." Second, as this attitude caught on in cities around the United States and beyond, prayer caught the attention of the church community and public at large. Thankfully, the resulting publicity, enthusiasm and unity drove more and more people to pray.

What role Concerts of Prayer plays in revival remains to be seen. One thing is clear: God has used David Bryant at a key, transitional moment to move Christians from "churchianity," the ritual of prayer, to organized, public forums in which the true need for prayer has been undeniable. People's longing for God has grown beyond organized meetings to more powerful expressions of prayer. And these expressions have brought believers to a new awareness of sin, a new day of repentance and a new spiritual awakening before God.

Pastors' Prayer Summits

One of the most powerful expressions of revival in our time has come through the Pastors' Prayer Summits, prompted by International Renewal Ministries in Portland, Oregon. I've already written how God, through this ministry, made a deep, profound affect on the pastors from Philadelphia in 1992. Their renewal is just one of many wonderful examples of the way God is using church leaders, many of whom feel broken and defeated, to breathe new, unexpected life into individual churches. Through Pastors' Prayer Summits, thousands of ministers have become life illustrations of revival for their own congregations. The ongoing story of this truly amazing work of God is the story of a man, a vision, and a movement that in many ways is still being born.

The date was January 19, 1992. The Portland Coliseum in Portland, Oregon, was "standing room only." Thirteen thousand, five hundred people had come, not to watch a pro basketball game, but to take part in a prayer meeting as the city looked ahead to the Pacific Northwest Billy Graham Crusade set for the following September. How could such an extraordinary expression of prayer happen in Oregon, the state with the highest percentage of people without a God-based value system in our nation? The only possible answer, of course, was "God." The "rest of the story" was how He had already been working years earlier through the man who prayed from the rostrum that night.

In the fall of 1988, Joe Aldrich found himself fifty miles south of the city at a pastor's breakfast in the nearby city of Salem.

"At the time, Portland and much of the surrounding area was so divided between the charismatic and non-charismatic communities," he remembers. "Pastors were discouraged, disheartened and fragmented. Though I sensed a willingness to reach out to each other, as pastors we were suspicious of each other, doctrinally divided. While there had been efforts to bring about reconciliation, I was unaware of any corporate expression.

"When I first came to Multnomah, I met with the board and told them my heart was for the Northwest and that Multnomah would be used as a catalyst for revival in the Northwest. I had met others in the city to whom the Lord had given a similar burden. Also, I began to see a couple of qualities that seemed to attract the blessing of God—unity and humility. I came to the conclusion that humility had to proceed unity."[18]

As he stood up to address the pastors in Salem that morning, Joe was thinking about a question that had reverberated within him for a long time.

"For fourteen or fifteen years I had asked the question, 'What would it take to initiate and sustain a work of God in a specific, geographical area?' Often I had wondered to myself, 'How do you get a group of people together to experience a humbling and a breaking, particularly pastors, when tradition and past divisions prevent them from reaching across denominational lines?' "[19]

That morning, Dr. Joe found the answer in the verse

he read aloud: "How good and pleasant it is when broth-ers live together in unity!" (Psalm 133:1). Then he asked the group, "Guys, what would it take for a bunch of us to get together?" Almost immediately, the pastors responded with a question of their own, "That's what we want. How do we do it?"

"I had been involved in pastors' conferences before," says Joe. "Often the participants would leave feeling tremendously blessed. They'd fly back home to their city, alone, without coming together with their fellow pastors where they lived."[20]

Several months after the Salem meeting, Joe added the practical exclamation mark to the pastors' response by inviting them and other ministers from the area to a con-ference center for a weekend retreat.

From the moment they arrived on Friday night, the men realized something was new.

"As a pastor in the early 1970s," Joe reflects, "I had done this with my own board of elders; I had organized a getaway Friday night and an all-day Saturday session, with no agenda but to praise God. As a result, my personal ministry just exploded with good things not because of anything I did. The participants on the weekend were 'one in Spirit' in the deepest sense I'd ever seen because we spent time with the Lord. It finally dawned on me to get these Salem-area pastors involved in the holiness of God, whatever it took."[21]

As a result, Joe made sure there was no keynote speak-er. He planned no special music. "In fact," he recalls, "there was not a single musical instrument! That week-end, we were willing to gamble and let the Spirit of God be the Spirit of God in our midst." That first Pastors' Prayer Summit could not have been scripted in advance because the events that unfolded over the next two days were totally unrehearsed and totally of God. In a very awesome way, Truth was stranger than fiction.

There was lots of time for singing, lots of time for prayer, lots of time for God to speak to ministers who were living a bad dream and who needed to be awakened.

"In one service," Aldrich recalls, "a pastor came to me during communion, grabbed my knee and said, 'Joe, there are seven churches that my church has grievously sinned against. I need to ask forgiveness of each of those pastors, personally.' After collecting himself, this pastor stood up before the gathering and said, 'My church has spoken against some of you and your ministries. That is wrong. We have sinned. Will you forgive me?'

"Not only was there forgiveness, but this one pastor's words touched off reciprocal confessions.

"Another time, we were just ready to start communion when a charismatic pastor stood up and said, 'I don't think any of us should take communion tonight. We know we've spoken against each other, we've undercut each other and we, of all people, should know that we are not to partake in an unworthy manner.' After that, pastor after pastor asked forgiveness of each other. I saw one charismatic pastor lying on the carpet, face down, crying to the Lord, 'I'm empty, I'm barren, I need to be filled and restored.'

"Confession before God is a great leveler among Christians," admits Joe. "Non-charismatic pastors had to admit, 'This charismatic knows his Bible. He loves The

Book. He loves the same songs I do. He's my brother!' On this extraordinary weekend the stereotypes, the prejudices that kept these fellow-Christian leaders apart for years, began to disappear."[22]

The word spread and several other Pastors' Prayer Summits were held within the next few months. Terry Dirks directs International Renewal Ministries, which fosters Pastors' Prayer Summits throughout the country. Observing the first few meetings, he says, "We began to see that God had placed in the hearts of His people a hunger for Himself. Men said, 'It's not business as usual. We don't need more seminars and conferences. We need a fresh touch of God in heaven-sent revival.'

"There was almost a feeling of desperation among the people. The Pacific Northwest had been characterized by a spirit of independence, rugged individualism and self-sufficiency. There had been a tremendous increase in gangs, violence and drugs. The region had been seen as a hot bed of the New Age Movement and even blatant demonic activity. It was enough for USA Today to refer to our area as a 'center of Godlessness'.[23]

"The pastors had finally become weary of saying, 'What are we going to do? We need a fresh touch of God.' I thought of Dennis Kinlaw who said, 'Your desperation is your greatest asset.' This is what we began to see during the first Pastors' Prayer Summits: when the people finally become desperate, we realize that we need God and we need each other. And that's when we began to see God move in new ways we had never seen before."

The format was simple, the outcome powerful. "Frequently, for the first couple of hours, all the participants were seated in a circle praising God," says Terry.

"What happened next was all spontaneous. One man would lead out in prayer verbally, or someone else would sing a song. All the songs were prayers themselves. This was singing to the Lord, not singing about Him.

"After two hours of praising God for who He is, we'd see a natural transition when someone would speak the words of Isaiah, 'Woe to me!' I cried, 'I am ruined! For I am a man of unclean lips, and I live among a people of unclean lips, and my eyes have seen the King, the Lord Almighty' (Isaiah 6:5).

"And then people would begin to confess their sin. We put a chair in the middle of the circle and said, 'If you have a real need to share with your brothers, come and share it and we'll gather around and pray for you.' One by one, men came confessing sins of pride, arrogance, competition, jealousy, lust, adultery, all of it spilling out as sewage from a drain pipe."

For Terry, seeing was believing.

"In the pastors I saw a hunger for God, His righteousness and His purity, more than I had ever seen before, resulting in incredible brokenness," he said. "Pastors confessed their sins to each other in real brokenness. There was humbling in individuals of a type I had never witnessed in my life. There was forgiveness from God and no condemnation between pastors. In that room I saw an unprecedented craving for God's holiness. I saw guys crying out to be men of purity. I saw reconciliation between pastors of different ministries and denominations taking place on the spot. One example of this stands out.

"A pastor sat down and for the next several minutes he wept like a baby. 'Guys,' he said, 'my marriage is on the rocks; I don't believe it's going to make it. My wife and I are basically two people living as roommates under the same roof, but there's no relationship. For years I've been married to the ministry, not to her. In twelve years of marriage I can count on one hand the number of times we've prayed together. When I go back home I don't know if she'll be there. It's all my fault.' He then put his head in his hands and began to cry some more.

"The other pastors cried as this man, sobbing between words, declared that if he told any of this to his church board he thought he'd be fired on the spot. Many of the men led out in prayer for their fellow pastor. One was a Southern Baptist pastor, several were from mainline denominations, others were Pentecostal. Then one of the men kneeling in front of this broken, distraught pastor, looked up into his eyes and said, 'Brother, when you go home, you may have to leave the ministry in order to put your family back together. If that happens, I want you to know that we will stand with you in whatever it takes; if it means paying for counseling or anything else. If you have to leave the ministry for awhile, if you need our support, we in the body of Christ in the city where you live will support you and your wife.'

"On the way home on the bus the men collected money for a weekend getaway for this man and his wife," says Terry. "Nine months later I received a letter from this pastor who had returned home from the weekend totally broken, renewed and unprepared for what was to come. He wrote:

Dear Terry,

I left the Pastors' Prayer Summit fully expecting that when I told my church board the things I shared that I'd be fired. Instead they responded wonderfully. As a result of my confession, those on the church board said, 'We too have already repented of things we've said and done. We too forgive you and we want to help you to see your marriage restored, and the church saved.'

A church that had been on a twenty-year decline has started to grow over the past nine months. A new Bible study group and a prayer group have started. Attendance on Sunday has increased 30 percent. Most of all, my marriage has been restored.

From the first gathering in February of 1989 through the end of 1994, nearly two hundred Pastors' Prayer Summits had been conducted.

"Through the Pastors' Prayer Summits I've experienced an awesome sense of God's holiness and righteousness," says Terry.

"I continue to be overwhelmed with the love of God and a sense of how God is bringing His people together in a true spirit of unity in ways I find it very difficult to describe.

"There is no desire for any man or organization to get the credit. There is only the awesome sense that this is of God. All of us working with the Pastors' Prayer Summits feel so privileged to be spectators, seeing what God is doing. When you know it's God, you're afraid to touch it for fear you'll get in the way and hinder something."[24]

Through the Pastors' Prayer Summits, I believe people such as Joe Aldrich, Terry Dirks and others have found a critical relationship between the initial stirrings of a fresh, spiritual awakening in America and what's needed to experience full-blown revival. If past revivals in our country are any indication of what's to come, the brokenness and restoration ministers are finding through the Pastors' Prayer Summits will lead to evangelism that brings others into a personal relationship with God through Jesus Christ.

Joe Aldrich captures the meaning of the Pastors' Prayer Summits in this powerful, articulate summation:

"In this movement we're watching, there is a desire to see God really impact a community. But to impact a community, we must be a community. To be a community we must have unity. To have unity we must have humility. And to have humility we must rediscover holiness."[25]

Community based on unity, unity built on humility, humility rooted in holiness.

This progression of faith sums up so well the way God is beginning to breathe new life into our nation's pastoral leaders—by bringing them to their knees through Pastors' Prayer Summits. The words of one summit participant suggest why these remarkable gatherings are synonymous with true "spiritual awakening." "We came to pray," he wrote, "but we beheld Jesus. I arrived as a pastor, I departed as a believer. No amount of words could explain the depth, the warmth, the love, the mutual care that has been imparted as we have looked to the Lord of the Church."

As ground-breaking as they've been, Pastors' Prayer Summits are merely a means for the current revival that's beginning to bubble in our land. As Terry Dirks suggests, the real focus, the *only* focus, needs to not be on a person involved in ministry but on the Person of Christ who's intimately involved in a reviving work of the Spirit.

Terry also sees the potential human hazards that could get in the way of what God has already begun.

"When God desires in His sovereign will to move upon His people in an unusual way," he says, "He'll raise up a person through whom He'll communicate that vision for what *He* wants to do; out of that flows a movement. The difficulty for many of us is that after a period of time, if we don't maintain that humble spirit of wanting to get out of the way, the flesh begins to enter in and we have people who want to somehow capture the excitement of that movement, market it or franchise it. In this way, things move from a man, to a movement, and finally to a machine that falls apart and becomes a monument."

By every indication so far, this is not what's happened to the Pastors' Prayer Summits. "It is true that God has raised up Joe Aldrich—not an organization, but as an organism," says Terry. "And there are other men of like mind, heart and passion.

"We are on the threshold of what could be a great spiritual awakening. Personally, I believe there will be a great spiritual awakening of the Church in America. The beginning signs are evident—conviction and brokenness over sin among church leaders, an overwhelming sense of the holiness of God, the tremendous joy over sins forgiven, and an awesome sense of the presence of Christ. All of those things are character traits of revivals. Soon it could be a fire that's out of man's control."[26]

Canadian Prayer Movement

In 1986, George Derksen was a fifty-three-year-old publisher from Toronto, Ontario, Canada. For years he had produced attractive magazines. Because he wanted to put his talents into something that people wouldn't throw away, he came up with an idea to produce a book unlike anything he had ever done. He designed *The Why Book* as an attractive, 150-page "coffee table book" to lead readers to ask the central question, "Why am I on this earth?" It was his way of reaching out with the Gospel. At Expo '86, the World's Fair in Vancouver, British Columbia, ten thousand copies of *The Why Book* were distributed at the Pavilion of Promise. Another one hundred thirty thousand copies were distributed throughout Winnipeg, Manitoba.

Two years later, a telepoll revealed startling findings:

- When asked if *The Why Book* was still in their home, 65 percent of the people said, "Yes."

- Sixteen percent said they had signed a commitment card (attached in the back of the book), to receive Jesus Christ as their personal Lord and Savior.

- The most remarkable discovery, however, was this: When those signing the commitment cards were asked if they had learned of anyone who had been praying for them, according to George, a majority said, "Yes, someone was praying."[27]

"Prayer had changed their responsiveness to the message," says George. "When people are not prayed for, they can sit like wooden soldiers. This was just the opposite."

Four years later, a group of church leaders in Toronto heard what happened in Winnipeg. They asked George if he would publish a similar book for the people in their city. "Knowing that prayer had been the foundation for God's saving work in Winnipeg, we knew there was no use going into Toronto without praying continuously," he says. "So we did. We prayed for a year. And finally we believed God was calling us to draw the Christians of Toronto together in united prayer."[28]

George then sent his business partner, Ann Wiens, to Toronto where she found three other women who began to fast and pray for others who would, in turn, pray for the people of this cosmopolitan city. A church-to-church campaign began, and by June of 1992, twenty-five thousand Christians in Toronto were using alphabetical lists in the local telephone directory to pray for every family in the city! No one had ever seen anything like it. The only thing to rival, and perhaps surpass, the scope and breadth of this grass-roots movement was a memorable, public expression of prayer. On June 22, 1992, twenty-eight thousand people gathered in Toronto's Sky Dome stadium for an unprecedented evening of prayer, worship and singing.

The response was so great that, several months later, George organized a team of three hundred and arranged a live satellite link-up that brought together sixty-five thousand Canadians in seven major stadia and meeting sites across Canada for the largest, simultaneous, cross-country prayer meeting in the country's history. The initial event is just one piece of a broad, spiritual mosaic now being fit together.

"Revival is breaking out in Canada," says George. "There's an openness to God in the churches and in government, a new hunger for God and a new hunger for prayer. It's a hunger I've not seen in my lifetime."[29]

- In Ottawa, Ontario, a group of 135 pastors meet each month to pray for revival.

- In London, Ontario, where seventeen hundred met to pray during the satellite prayer session, men are phoning other men to pray for them. The calls last fifteen, sometimes thirty minutes.

- In Winnipeg, Manitoba, where people have been praying more intentionally for spiritual awakening since 1987, more than six hundred people have come to Christ through two evangelistic meetings. In one service alone, four hundred people stood up and walked toward the altar to profess their faith in the risen Lord. According to George Derksen, Senior Pastor Dr. H.H. Barber gave a call for baptism and thirty others were baptized by immersion in their street clothes. Derksen said the pastor remarked, "In forty years I've never seen anything like it."[30]

- At a normally-reserved church in Niverville, Manitoba, south of Winnipeg, a woman stood up to give her testimony as part of her baptismal service. The pastor called for others to come forward. One man with a less-than-admired reputation stood up and said, "You all know what I've been like in this town. I ask you to forgive my sins."

- In the town of Barrie, Ontario, north of Toronto, a woman made prayer a daily habit. Each morning she would walk by each of the homes in her neighborhood. At each house she stopped and prayed for each parent and child and asked the Lord to save them. *Within the next year members from each of the ten families accepted Christ!*

"My prayer is that God will revive the people of Canada and save our country," says George.[31] My prayer is that Canada will be known as a country of prayer." And, he could add, as a country that is coming to Christ in a manner both Canadians and Americans, perhaps, have just begun to see.

A Special Call to Prayer & Fasting for Our Country

"I am convinced that God will soon send a great spiritual awakening to our country and the world. . . ."[32]

The words came from Bill Bright, founder and director of Campus Crusade for Christ International. In a warm yet urgent three-page letter, Bill had invited Christian leaders in the United States to join him from December 5-7, 1994, for three days of prayer and fasting in Orlando, Florida.

The names of seventy-two distinguished Christian men and women who made up the Invitation Committee told me that this gathering would be a first in recent memory. But it was Bill's own story that convinced me I had to attend:

For me, the call to fast and pray for our nation began in earnest on July 5, 1994, when I began a 40-day fast for revival and awakening in America and the fulfillment of the Great Commission throughout the world. On the morning that I began my twenty-ninth day of fasting I was reading in 2 Chronicles, chapters 28-30, when God's holy Word spoke to my heart in a most unusual way.

Like ancient Judah, our nation is rapidly becoming morally and spiritually destitute. As I read that Hezekiah, King of Judah, wrote a letter to the leaders of Israel and Judah inviting them to join him in celebrating the Passover in the newly opened, cleansed and dedicated temple—which his evil father, Ahaz, had closed—I felt impressed by the Lord to write letters to hundreds of the most influential Christians in this country, inviting them to gather in Orlando, as guests of Campus Crusade, to fast and pray. We do not have a political agenda.

This will be strictly a time for fasting and prayer and for seeking God's direction on how we, His servants, can be instruments of revival for our nation and the world.

By God's grace, this could be one of the most significant prayer and fasting gatherings in modern history.[33]

I accepted Bill's invitation and went to Florida. Based on all that happened in Orlando, I can say that, by God's grace, Bill's hope and prayer came true. As one of nearly seven hundred participants, I witnessed an unusual display of Christian leaders across the denominational and parachurch spectrum. That unity was expressed best by author/speaker Kay Arthur who gave the memorable illustration of two different heart tissues beating at different rhythms, yet when they physically touch each other, they beat in unison. "When we touch Jesus," she says, "we pump the same."

Throughout the three days of fasting and praying in Orlando, it was clear that many, many Christian leaders have been praying for God to bring revival to our land. In that sense, Orlando was not so much a new beginning but the continuation of a journey. Steve Hall, a prayer leader from Seattle, summed it up well: "The meeting in Orlando was one more step in what God has been doing for years. God has been birthing a deep hunger for Himself in ministers, leaders and in cities for at least the past ten to twenty years. Today, more and more of these people are saying, 'There's such a desperation in our world, it's time we got on our faces with one another to break down barriers and build bonds of love and trust.' "[34]

One speaker offered an illuminating illustration of this by telling the story of Luther, who in the midst of a conflict with Zwingli, went into the mountain country one day. Luther saw a narrow path on which one mountain goat was going down while another was going up. Obviously there was not room for both. Luther wondered what would happen. It seemed impossible that both goats could continue their journey. Curiosity gave way to astonishment. With the two animals face-to-face, the goat going up the hill knelt down and allowed the descending goat to walk over his back.

What a picture of submission and common cause! Seeking Christ during this time of emerging revival will mean we'll not only have to give up our individuality, we may also need to let others walk on our back; we may simply have to die to self.

Flickering Lights in a Darkening World

Seven hundred Christians leaders fasting and praying together for three days in Orlando, Florida.

A handful of tired pastors meeting for breakfast in Salem, Oregon.

An even smaller group of ten men meeting in a church building before work in Davenport, Iowa.

One person, Nell Barr, getting up at six o'clock in the morning to pray with her husband.

The stirring power of prayer in America today is defined by everyday people such as these. The significance of revival prayer is found in such small pockets of individuals like Nell, now coming to God in the cold morning dawn while most of us are still asleep. In the history of spiritual awakening, God has never used a majority for good reason—that way He gets all the glory. He's awakening believers across the United States and in Canada through a *few faithful people of prayer*. It's the same thing He did nearly fifty years ago.

It happened on the Hebrides Islands off the western

coast of Scotland in 1947. A group of five to seven very godly men had become concerned about their home and country. Sadly, they felt that the Spirit of God was absent. They were despondent about their friends' indifference to the Gospel and their nation's indifference to spiritual things. These men realized that the needs were so far beyond them that their only hope, their only answer, was to go before God.

So, sacrificially, these few common men began to pray. After working all day, they would go home for dinner and dedicate the evening to their families. Then, around ten o'clock, when they were tired and ready to go to bed, they would walk out into the night and meet together in a lighted barn. And there they would pray. Sometimes five of them, sometimes six, sometimes seven. For two long years they went to the barn, night after night. In the heat of summer and in the briskness of fall, in the chill of winter and in the cool of spring, these sacrificing, godly men met together. On their knees.

"Oh, God," they cried out, "do something for our islands."

Every time they prayed they always read a passage of Scripture, and they prayed until they had peace in their hearts. Then, one night in 1949, two years after they had begun meeting, as they gathered in the barn, one of the men opened his Bible to Psalm 24 and began to read. "The earth is the Lord's, and the fulness thereof; the world, and they that dwell therein. For he hath founded it upon the seas, and established it upon the floods. Who shall ascend into the hill of the Lord? Or who shall stand in his holy place? He that hath clean hands, and a pure heart; who hath not lifted up his soul unto vanity, nor sworn deceitfully" (Psalm 24:1-4, KJV).

Suddenly the truth hit these men. "Is it possible," they asked, "that for two, long years we've been praying night after night, sacrificially, for the Lord to move on our islands—and yet our hands are not clean? Is it possible our hearts are not pure? Is it possible that our souls have been lifted up to vanity and that we have sworn deceitfully?" That moment, the Lord convicted them that all the things they feared were true. That night, they prayed the words from the Book of James, "Therefore, confess your sins to each other and pray for each other so that you may be healed. The prayer of a righteous man is powerful and effective" (5:16).

History records that these men left the barn that night and on the way to the village, they topped the hill. They looked down the road. There, in the ditch, they saw two town drunks on their knees, stumbling and mumbling. But as the believers came closer they realized they weren't drunk at all, they were sober. And they were praying; they were on their knees, under conviction of sin, asking God to forgive them.

"The prayer of a righteous man is powerful and effective."

The men who had prayed every night for months looked out over the night sky and saw the homes below. At 1:30 A.M., lights in the village were on. The people had awakened from their sleep. Dozens of families, realizing their separation from God, had gotten up from their beds in consternation to try to find someone awake with whom they could talk. Night became dawn, and the next morning people knew that something had changed. The people invited Duncan Campbell, the great evangelist from England, to visit their homeland. He came, preached, and great revival broke out, a revival that was born through prayer in a barn.[35]

"Oh God, do something for our nation."

This is the voice of prayer. This is the voice of Christians in small-town Montana, big-city New York, and hundreds of living rooms and sanctuaries in between who've run out of answers, though not out of faith. This is the steady plea of church-goers who long for something better than what they find in the newspaper and in their own lives. This is the cry of pastors ready to unload years of hidden, unconfessed sin into the arms of their forgiving colleagues and loving Lord.

"Oh God, do something . . ."

This is the voice of believers who want an end to the spiritual emptiness they feel in their own lives and in their nation. This is the voice of weariness, anger, and longing. This is the voice of people who feel dead inside and who want to live again, who have run out of human explanations and have only one option.

"Oh God . . . "

This is where revival begins and how it will grow in our country. God is stirring His people to pray. Why then should we be surprised that the first sprinkles of revival are being felt in the United States and in Canada? *Why, when men and women have been praying for this very thing for years?* If God could use the prayers of a handful of men to awaken the faith of a disbelieving village, what do you think He could do with the prayers of thousands of men and women in North America who are praying right now for their own respective nations?

What do you think God could do in your life, your church, your nation, if you began praying for revival? No one knows the answer—yet. But one thing is absolutely certain:

If the moral deterioration, violence and greed in our nation grieves you;

If the growing indifference to the Gospel of salvation saddens you;

If the break-up of marriages, families and other cherished relationships hurts you;

If these and other sorrows have stirred a new hunger for God, a new need to pray in you—

You are not alone. Call it a movement. Call it a new spiritual awakening. Call it what you will. If your prayer is that our nation turn from its prodigal ways and come home to a loving Father who's ready to pour out His goodness and love, then you are already a part of something new, something starting to unfold. If your heart beats in unison with the people you've been reading about, then you are part of the Pastors' Prayer Summits. You are part of Nell Barr's early morning prayer time. You are part of the group of workers who meet before work to pray for their city, country and church.

You are already part of revival!

If your response is "Yes," if you are filled with expectation and hope for all that God is now unfolding in North America and all that is yet to come, be glad. *And be aware*. The current spiritual awakening is not without potential obstacles. Some are glaring menaces. Others are so subtle, so ingrained in our way of life, you may not recognize them even though they could be the very reasons for either your own spiritual malaise or your impatience and frustration that God isn't doing more to bring our nation to repentance and healing. That's why we need to take a closer look at what could be inhibiting the awakening that's already begun.

Endnotes

1. Charles G. Finney, *Lectures on Revival of Religion* (New York: Fleming H. Revell, 1988), 22-34.

2. Nell Barr, telephone conversation, 28 November, 1994.

3. Larry Mancini, telephone conversation, 28 October 1994.

4. Paul Fleischmann, telephone conversation, 22 November 1994.

5. Ibid.

6. James W. Tharp, letter, 28 February 1994.

7. Nell Barr, telephone conversation, 28 November 1994.

8. James W. Tharp, letter, 15 November 1994.

9. James W. Tharp, letter, 28 February 1994.

10. Ibid.

11. Nell Barr, telephone, 28 November 1994.

12. Ibid.

13. Ibid.

14. Duane Vaughn, telephone conversation, 28 November 1994.

15. "Mission Statement" (Concerts of Prayer International, Wheaton, Illinois, 1994), 1.

16. "What is a 'Concert of Prayer?' " Concerts of Prayer newsletter (Concerts of Prayer International, Wheaton, Illinois, 1993), 2.

17. Ibid.

18. Joe Aldrich, telephone conversation, 8 February 1994.

19. Ibid.

20. Ibid.

21. Ibid.

22. Ibid.

23. Terry Dirks, telephone conversation, 4 February 1994.

24. Ibid.

25. Joe Aldrich, telephone conversation, 8 February 1994.

26. Terry Dirks, telephone conversation, 4 February 1994.

27. George Derksen, telephone conversation, 6 December 1994.

28. Ibid.

29. Ibid.

30. Ibid.

31. Ibid.

32. Bill Bright, letter, 7 October 1994, 2.

33. Ibid.

34. Steve Hall, telephone conversation, 7 December 1994.

35. Colin C. Whittaker, *Great Revivals* (Gospel Publishing House, Springfield, Mo., 1984) 181-183.

CHAPTER SIX

Unseen Obstacles Ahead

If anyone has his finger on the pulse of the current revival stirrings in North America, it may be Dr. Lewis Drummond. This respected, godly scholar has written several noted books on revival and has held the Billy Graham Chair of Evangelism at Beeson Divinity School (Samford University) in Birmingham, Alabama, since 1991. I met Dr. Drummond in 1976 at the Southern Baptist Theological Seminary in Louisville, Kentucky, where he was then teaching. At the time, talk of spiritual awakening in this country was almost nil. "There was not near as much interest in revival or prayer back then as there is today," he recalls.[1]

Today, more than eighteen years later, Dr. Drummond

is seeing the kind of revival stirrings that preceded our nation's Great Awakenings.

"I'm seeing at least two things I've never seen in my lifetime, two things that make me think America may be ripe for a new spiritual awakening," he says. "First, there's never been so much concern and interest in revival. I'm seeing this renewed interest in pastors, and to some extent, in laypersons as well.

"The second thing that's remarkable about the potential for revival in America is the increasing interest in prayer and the formation of prayer groups we're seeing throughout our nation. Though it's still in the developmental stage, there's so much prayer for revival today. Again, I've never seen anything quite like it in my lifetime."[2]

Pastors' Prayer Summits. Concerts of Prayer. One million youth meeting annually around their schools' flagpoles to pray for their teachers, their fellow-students, and their country. Thousands of men meeting weekly in Promise Keepers' small groups and finding a new, humble awareness of what it means to love and serve their wives, their children and most of all, their God. High-profile movements such as the historic meeting "A Special Call to Prayer & Fasting for Our Country" in Orlando, Florida.

All of them are bringing Christians together in an urgent, uncommon fellowship. For every magazine cover headline like the one in *Newsweek* (November '94) that announced "The Search for the Sacred: America's Quest for Spiritual Meaning," there's an increasing number of Christians who've found new meaning as they pray for revival. From the most highly organized movement in the spotlight of the national media to the quietest church gathering you or I will never know about, people are desiring a new breath of God for their individual lives, their cities and their nation.[3]

When it comes to revival, the question many of these Christians, including Lewis Drummond and myself, are asking is, "Where will it all lead? How close could our country be to a full-blown, national awakening?" When you read about one million junior and senior high school students praying in front of their schools with fellow students and administrators looking on, it's hard not to be excited by the extraordinary ways God is causing His people to hunger and pray for spiritual awakening.

Yet, genuine enthusiasm is a double-edged sword. In the coming days, all of the interest, desire and prayers for God to revive our land could become nothing more than the spiritual equivalent of "one step forward, two steps back"—if we don't see the very real, unseen obstacles to revival that are in our midst. Whether America's next Great Awakening is coming next year or in the next century, every Christian who prays for revival will face these obstacles sooner or later. In fact, the potential barriers I'm thinking of are so deceptively present, I believe they could be keeping you and me from seeing, perhaps even experiencing, what God is doing in our nation right now.

Hindering Revival: It's Happened Before

The obstacles I'm painfully aware of lurk in the enthusiasm of well-intentioned Christians who genuinely want more of God. Lewis Drummond articulates what has happened in the church today:

"At one stage in my ministry, I preached on 2 Chronicles 7:14, ' . . . if my people, who are called by my name, will humble themselves and pray and seek my face and turn from their wicked ways, then will I hear from heaven and will forgive their sin and will heal their land.' I stressed that if you do these things—humble, pray, seek God's face and turn from your wicked ways—you will have a revival. In actuality, these things are not the *prerequisites* to revival, they *are* the revival; the forgiving of sins, healing of land, are the results.

"But here's what I think has happened. Though individually we're to humble ourselves, pray, seek God's face and turn from our wicked ways, many Christians, particularly pastors, have fallen into what author, preacher and theologian Stephen Olford calls 'evangelical humanism'. This is a determined, well-meaning faith that says, 'We can do this thing! We can grow our church! We can be the people God wants us to be.' Such an 'if/then' approach says, 'If you do these five things, God's blessing is bound to happen.' While humility, prayer, seeking after God and repenting from our wickedness are things God calls us to do, merely trying to 'work them out the best we can' may stand in the way of real revival."[4]

How can this be possible? How can a true spiritual awakening, inspired and sustained by God, be derailed by faithful, well-meaning believers? Is it possible that you and I could stand in the way of how God is reviving the faith and life of Christians across our land?

Though God is sovereign, the present and emerging spiritual awakening in our land could, in fact, be stilled prematurely. This movement of the Holy Spirit could be hindered by men and women who stiffen at any unusual occurrence that doesn't fit their ordinary religious tradition. This movement of the Spirit could be hindered by believers who are afraid to learn the vulnerable truth about their own rusted, sinful cores that can only be cleaned out and cleaned up by the most vulnerable act of all: by admitting that our corrosion, our sin, is choking off the flow of the Spirit. And it may not be "the other guy" who's hindering revival. Well-meaning Christians—you and I—could resist being vulnerable to God to the point that we could hinder the Holy Spirit's movement, and thus hinder revival.

It's happened before.

Drummond observed how in the early 1960s the Spirit was cut short in a free church in England. "During worship on this particular Sunday, I saw people being convicted of their own brokenness and sin. They really began to weep. The pastor may have been unfamiliar with the work of the Spirit, or he may have just been plain scared to death, because he put a stop to the people's expressiveness. He chastised these confessing Christians for their tears and in so doing curtailed the awakening work of the Spirit in the congregation."[5]

A second instance of revival cut short took place closer to home. Drummond recalls when revival began to break out at a theological seminary in the United States. Unrelated to the Spirit's movement on campus, one student who was either demonic or psychotic said to his peers one day, "I'm going to get on the roof of the men's dormitory, and I'll jump off and float down to the ground and bring a great revival." Notes Drummond, "It was the identical temptation of Jesus on the pinnacle of the Temple. Except this young man didn't float. He fell hard to the ground and broke his legs. The incident alarmed the administration. Instead of realizing this was a satanic attack, they stopped all prayer groups for revival."[6]

Let me be clear about this: God is sovereign, and His will, "will be done." God wants to bring spiritual awakening to His people, an awakening you and I need to see, the real creation He's set before us. A living analogy shows why.

If you and I slept twenty-four hours a day without awakening, how would we ever see this wonderful planet God has created for us? Similarly, if we never were awakened spiritually, how could we see the true life of joy, fulfillment and blessing that God has before us as individuals and corporately as a nation?

As a slumbering Church, as individuals indifferent to our own spiritual fatigue, we're missing the sunlight of the day with Christ. We're missing the wonderful meals we could be having with Him. We're missing the fellowship with other believers that could be so unbelievably fulfilling and joyous. We're missing a little bit of heaven on earth. In short, we could be our own worst obstacles to the awakening we so desperately need and want. And we don't even know it.

True spiritual awakening that once turned our nation back to God (and may turn us to Him again) will take place once more because God chooses to love human beings who choose to receive Him. The only thing that can possibly stand in the way of the next Great Awakening (and it's a big "only"), the only obstacle to experiencing revival in all its fullness, will be if you and I are unwilling or unable to receive the blessing God is ready to give. You and I won't hinder revival because we stand in the way of an all-powerful, all-caring God, but because we simply aren't willing to receive the great love He wants to pour out. If you're concerned about possible obstacles to revival, don't expect to find a satisfying "answer" in the eternal, theological tug-of-war of God's sovereignty vs. man's free will. The relevant questions we need to be asking are these:

"Do I want to be part of an extraordinary movement of the Holy Spirit in this nation?"

"Do I long for God's forgiveness and healing in this country, a movement that can come only from Him?"

If your answer to both is yes, if deeper spiritual life is what you seek, then be ready to experience two very distinct and opposing forces. The first is God's infinite desire to bring our nation to Himself. The second is your own imperfect nature that causes you to look out for self. It's in this flawed, human interior where the potential obstacles to revival dwell. To know these three obstacles that could keep you from personal revival—and our nation from a genuine spiritual awakening—you need only look at your own heart.

The first potential obstacle to personal and national spiritual revival is as basic as our desire to know God. It is the need to understand.

North Americans are influenced strongly by the Greek, rationalistic tradition that says, in effect, that the most effective way of knowing something or someone is through the mind. The mind is the avenue of knowledge, the mechanism on which we depend to know ourselves, others, our world and our God. This rationalistic heritage is so embedded in who we are that we often make our analytical thinking processes synonymous with belief. Thus our faith tends to follow a logical, rational path. If we want to know who God is and what He's about, we:

- *Observe*—become aware of all that's in and around us.
- *Take in*—receive all the data we can gather.
- *Organize*—arrange the assorted thoughts, feelings and questions.
- *Analyze*—look closely to sort out what we want to accept or reject.
- *Understand*—conclude "what's real, what's true, what we can use."

Rick Marshall is not a person to rely on experience alone. Yet at the Cannon Beach Christian Conference Center where approximately ten Philadelphia pastors joined 150 other ministers working on the Billy Graham Crusade in Portland, his life was literally renewed. This man—who knew the Word extremely well, who received training from the Navigators, who had always approached things from a clear, rationalistic perspective—*experienced* the Holy Spirit. This gifted young leader, who had always come to a knowledge of faith and truth through reason, finally came to a more expressive understanding of who God is through conviction, confession and repentance. In his letter to Joe Aldrich after the meeting, Rick describes far better than I can what happened to him:

Words are inadequate to express how I feel before the Lord, having had the privilege of joining you and the brothers from Oregon in the recent prayer summit. My story is as follows: each day, Monday, Tuesday and Wednesday, I felt the hand of God heavy upon me. Every man that sat in the chair was me. Yet my pride prevented me from getting right with God.

Thursday morning I felt I could not return to Philadelphia without an opportunity to publicly make a confession. To my delight and freedom, we had one more session on Thursday morning, as the Lord so graciously provided with the brothers from Philadelphia. Before these men I was able to release my burden and weight of sin. Alleluia![7]

The convicting power of God that Rick experienced certainly did not negate his God-given ability to reason; it simply affirmed the principles of the Word that he already knew and now fulfilled. One of those was "Be still and know that I am God" (Psalm 46:10). Rick heard that "still, small voice" (1 Kings 19:12), and confessed his sin, for which he received forgiveness. And God broke through! Rick realized that knowledge wasn't all. What changed him was person-to-person contact with God through the power of the Holy Spirit. This experiential reality simply built upon and confirmed the true meaning of "conviction"—"to see as God sees." And only the Holy Spirit, far beyond what the human, rational mind could ever comprehend, could allow Rick to see himself as God sees him—sinful, forgiven and loved.

By relying primarily on our rationalistic, western

minds, we limit our understanding of revival; we also might be led to some unforeseen, absurd conclusions. Few people realize that the human mind has a rational element that tends to be irrational. The flaw comes from the Fall. Prior to the Fall, the mind as a means of spiritual communication with God was complete and perfect. Reason, therefore, was also perfect. Today what we lift up as "reason" is flawed because some of our ability to comprehend, understand, express and communicate with God has been damaged. (This will be the case until you and I are reunited with Him and made complete with Him in heaven.) In our absurd egos, we're not wise enough to understand the fallacy of the boast that our minds are the highest of all reason.

Because of the Fall, faith was stripped away from reason. Yet faith is a vital part of complete, perfect reason. A man or woman without God has flawed reason when not exercising faith ("the substance of things hoped for, the evidence of things not seen," Hebrews 11:1). God's reason has an element in it that can not be grasped empirically. There's a Reason above human reason that features the element of faith. Without faith, what the human mind concludes can become absurd. That's why, if one takes any theological concept and carries it to an "ultimate reasonable conclusion," as some theologians have done, perceived truth can become an absurdity.

Charles Finney, for example, laid out what he referred to as his "Principles (or Measures) of Revival" (not to be mistaken for his "Seven Indicators" referred to earlier). Finney believed that if Christians followed through with these "Principles," God had no choice but to bring spiritual awakening. In Finney's latter years, some of his followers were doing everything their mentor said to do, including praying for people by name in public and having open or "protracted" meetings. Finney's measures were quite rational—yet the people did not experience revival. Finney himself went to one specific church, led the people in the principles, and revival *did* occur. The reason God brought spiritual awakening was because He had called Finney to be the personification of revival, not because of the rational make-up of the principles themselves.[8]

It's absurd to expect that practicing any set of points can lead even the most faithful, well-intentioned Christian to a spiritual awakening. This is not to be critical of Finney. The point is this: relying solely on rationalistic knowledge will always lead believers to incomplete and, in some cases, invalid conclusions that fall well short of true revival.

Simply put, our flawed, rationalistic minds cannot fully comprehend revival. Revival is not a mystery to be "thought through"; it is a movement of the Spirit to be experienced with reverence, checked against the clear guidelines of Scripture, and then given to the God who alone deserves our praise. If we want to know this God, particularly in a season of awakening, we need to remember Jesus' words: "God is spirit, and his worshipers must worship in spirit and in truth" (John 4:24).

How can we know the Spirit with organized, yet limited rationalistic minds? How can we use our minds to the fullest to understand revival, without limiting our understanding of God to what our minds can process? As you come to God through your own prayer, confession and repentance, come to him not with the Greek mindset that compartmentalizes life into body, soul, and spirit. Come to God with the mindset of the Hebrew, as a whole person made complete in God.

The Hebrew mindset did not compartmentalize body, mind and soul. None of the three was any more or less important than the other two. All three comprised the one person. Our emotion, a vital part of one's soul to the Hebrew (distinct from emotionalism, which can be manufactured), would be as vital a part of your make-up as your mind. Rick Marshall could look at the Word of God and know what sin is. He could comprehend and identify sin. But only when Rick's personal emotions—the center of his being—were touched by the Holy Spirit, only when he saw himself as God saw him, only when he had disdain for the ungodly things in his life, could he be awakened. The same is true for you and me. Personal revival occurs when we allow God to have preeminence through the mind (knowledge), the body (obedience) and the soul (confession).

Our need to understand can move us in one of two directions. We can come to rely on God chiefly through our ability to reason; or we can seek God, knowing that our faith can never be measured exclusively by the rational benchmark of "what makes sense."

The first potential obstacle to revival is allowing ourselves to be satisfied with our desire to know *about* God when our real need is to *experience* God in mind, body and soul, and so be brought to life by Him and through Him. With our minds we can *realize this fact through His Word* and by *experiencing the Living Word*. The two go together. Realizing there is so much more the Spirit can teach us, we can use our minds as a gateway to learning, a tool that can help us analyze the other barriers that could keep us from experiencing the next Great Awakening in our land.

A *second potential obstacle to personal and national spiritual awakening is the very real fear of not being accepted (and being rejected) by others.*

In an age of conformity, the thought of speaking out and standing up for God can be a truly ominous barrier.

Imagine experiencing a new, deep sense of your own brokenness and your utter need for forgiveness and holiness. Imagine God being so real, so close, so alive that you begin to devour the Scriptures with a voracious desire to know this God in a way you've never known. As you grow to know Him more, sins you once rationalized or ignored now feel like damaging, personal affronts to your best friend. You admit to God your own desire to keep sinning even while you find a new willingness to turn your back on old patterns and walk in a new direction toward God. This 180-degree turnaround is true repentance. When people want to know "What's different with you?" you know the answer, and a thousand thoughts go through your mind, among them:

What is he or she going to think about me once I start talking about God?

I don't even have words to describe something I've never known, even though I'm convinced it's of God. What will I say?

I'm afraid she's not going to understand.

I'm afraid he won't accept me.

185

*This spiritual renewal is so new, so real, so personal,
I'm not sure I feel comfortable bringing it up.*

This is the voice of wanting to be accepted. This is the deep human need to be liked by others. This is the willingness to be accepted even if it means silencing the undeniable truth that God is alive and at work in us.

I know the sound of this voice too well, because when I look at the list of possible excuses above, I hear Tom Phillips speaking. Ever since I was a young seminary student I've never had much of a problem opening my mouth to talk about God—except when it involved possible rejection. In twenty-plus years of ministry centered largely in evangelism, I've had literally thousands of opportunities to proclaim the wonderful salvation message of Christ to others. Yet there are still times when, even though I know I'm telling the Truth, even when I know I'm helping someone go from darkness to light and from hell to heaven, I admit to myself, *I don't want to be rejected.* At these times my personal fear of not being accepted overrides my love for the person and the place of their eternal soul.

Though I am chagrined to admit this, I also know that I'm not alone. In fact, the reality of revival in our time raises this anxiety of personal rejection to new levels.

In Buenos Aires, Argentina, in the summer of 1992, I was one of more than a thousand believers packed inside a Baptist church for a pre-Billy Graham Crusade meeting. That evening God's Spirit began to move mightily in ways I had never observed. One moment people were standing in the aisles lifting their hands in praise to God. The next moment they were dropping to the floor without anyone touching them—catatonic!

I saw this happen all around the room. There was no rhyme or reason why these men and women were falling to the floor except that they were feeling a powerful touch of the Holy Spirit. I should have been celebrating this great work of God! Instead I became terribly anxious inside. *Oh God, please don't touch me like that,* I thought, looking around quickly at people on either side who had fallen to the floor and were still seemingly unconscious. Instead of praising God, I worried. *Oh God, don't let this happen to me. I don't want to be embarrassed!*

The great revivals in history have spread because the people God touched couldn't keep His awesome presence and power to themselves. Telling their fellow believers and unbelieving neighbors about the Lord who had breathed new life into them came quite naturally. Did the thought of looking like a fool, of being rejected by others, ever cross their minds? Perhaps. Yet the large numbers of conversions and increased church membership tell me that their "fear over what others may think" was no obstacle to revival.

In 1970 small groups of students fanned out across our nation from Asbury College in Wilmore, Kentucky. They had just completed a chapel service that began on Tuesday morning, February 3. The dean of the college, the scheduled speaker that day, did not feel impressed to preach. Instead, he felt led to have students participate in a testimony meeting. For the next seven days, twenty-four hours a day, one student or faculty member after another went to the platform, broken by the Lord, and told his or her story. There was confession, weeping, shouting—and praising of God.

What occurred at Asbury was true revival. It spread

everywhere the students went, declaring what God was doing in their lives. They were not ashamed of what they had seen and experienced. When they spoke to others, awakening broke out all over again.[9] This was true in seminaries such as the Southwestern Southern Baptist Theological Seminary in Fort Worth, Texas, and to some degree at Southern Seminary in Louisville, Kentucky.[10]

The reawakening that is to come and that may already be here won't hinge on whether today's image-conscious Christians go public with their convictions. God doesn't need to do an end-run around people's anxiety to be heard. I wonder how many of the one million teenage students who met for public prayer at their schools' flagpoles felt self-conscious by what their non-praying friends thought? For God, our lack of courage is not an ultimate obstacle to revival, but an opportunity to work through fragile egos and sweaty palms. So whether it's in a church in Argentina or in your own congregation, we can know that our need for human affirmation and acceptance is no obstacle for a God who is not ashamed to be seen with us. Even though He knows we are flawed vessels, He is ready to pour His Spirit into those who are willing to acknowledge the Potter and be remade by Him.

A third potential obstacle to personal and national spiritual awakening is apathy.

This disease of disinterest has been a nagging, disruptive gadfly to every revival in our nation's history. Apathy can take one of two forms: either a gradual familiarity with the extraordinary movement of the Holy

Spirit; or an overt disinterest in undeniable and extraordinary works of God. The first kind takes the form of a subtle comfort that breeds spiritual boredom and fatigue. The second kind is an overt disregard in caring about the obvious.

The first kind of apathy, a kind of spiritual descent of the heart, is one of the chief reasons that, without exception, nearly all revivals in history have never lasted more than a generation. Think of watching a spectacular Fourth of July fireworks display. We are awed by the first colorful explosions, entertained by the next few bursts, but bored by the time it's over. Though the explosions grow more spectacular, more elaborate, our interest wanes. At first we think this is the greatest thing we've ever witnessed. After awhile, when we've seen enough, we just want to get back to the car and beat the traffic home. Likewise, the intensity and wonder of past spiritual awakenings have left Christians awed, interested and finally apathetic over time. It's true that, by God's design, revivals are not continuous. It's also true that, from Moses' time to today, God's followers can only take so much of His extraordinary outpouring before familiarity prompts loss of interest.

The only exception to this kind of short-term involvement with revival (at least of which I'm aware) took place in the spiritual awakening that came to the Rwanda Valley in Uganda in the early 1950s. This extraordinary movement of the Spirit lasted nearly two generations. One possible reason is that apathy was not allowed to fester.

According to Dr. Drummond, when a Christian met someone on the path in the morning, he or she would say,

"Good morning, brother," or "Good morning, sister. Is your cup running over?" If the person answered yes, then the other would say, "Praise God." If the person said no, then the one who initiated the conversation would ask, "What then, my brother or sister, is the matter?" Almost without exception, the troubled individual would take the time and confess right there on the spot the specific concern or sin before God and his or her fellow believer. He or she would then receive forgiveness and go on his or her way, cleansed and rejoicing. Imagine what would have happened if people had not let their love for God "spill over" into their everyday greetings, had they not been willing to ask "What's the matter?"[11] Because of the people's overt love for Christ and for each other, others' subtle apathy toward sin wasn't allowed to flourish.

The second form of apathy is the overt variety that works against revival before spiritual awakening has had a chance to emerge. This is the kind of apathy you hear today:

Revival? Taking place today? Never heard about it.

Revival? Isn't that what they do at tent meetings with wild, screaming preachers?

Revival seems like something out of history. What good have revivals ever done?

Revival? Isn't that what evangelistic meetings held twice-a-year in the South are called?

This kind of apathy erodes people's openness and anticipation for what God is already beginning to do in our land. More than indifference, apathy has the potential to blossom into true lack of concern, jealousy, and even antagonism. It's not a big stretch of the imagination to hear these voices speak out against even the mere possibility of a new, uncontained spiritual awakening:

Don't bother me. What if this is not real? If I stick out my neck prematurely and this thing embarrasses me, it could ruin my ministry.

You think I'm going to admit to my own people that I've got overt sin in my life? You think I'm going to lay myself open to criticism and alienation by confessing it openly?

How can I possibly admit to my church that I'm not the spiritual leader that they think I am?

I can hear these kinds of fears from pastors, though the same human inhibitions and excuses apply to lay persons as well. The obstacle of apathy and the antagonism it can foster relate to the drastic change revival always brings. Christian leaders, particularly those in high-profile ministries, don't like change because change disturbs the status quo. Change threatens administrative systems and fund-raising campaigns. True change, change brought about by the Spirit, becomes threatening when people begin to direct their attention away from a ministry or a leader and toward the wonderful work of the Spirit.

When the leader happens to personify that revival spirit, apathy from other Christian leaders can turn to outright jealousy. An unfortunate harbinger of revival is found in the saying that "Grace bestowed always leads to jealousy." Why? Because grace is always unmerited. Show me the person who's received unmerited acknowledgment and honor, and I'll show you an excuse for jealousy. Look at Joseph in the Old Testament. Were his brothers peeved that his dad gave him the coat of many colors because he was his daddy's favorite son? Yes! But what really made the brothers jealous was his description of his dreams, given to him by God, in which they bowed to him. They had been the ones who worked hard, who led their families, who sacrificed by spending nights out in the cold watching the sheep. Then to be told by a kid wearing a multicolored coat, "You're going to bow to me someday!"

When God inspires the "Josephs" of our day to personify the new, unfolding work of the Spirit, there will be plenty of jealous "obstacles" standing by to offer their unsolicited opinions. If they are not apathetic or antagonistic, they will be merely reticent to jump on board. Conventional wisdom says, "Better to be a lukewarm defender by standing back and observing revival from afar than to seek God in the unseen assurance that is faith. That way, without risking reputation, you can gain from the new because the new might not succeed, and you'd end up with mud on your face. Better to wait and be sure."

The result of apathy and its antagonistic cousins is that pastors who have been play-acting are going to be brought down. Who will be lifted up? Perhaps humble, spiritually mature pastors and lay leaders who seek God, without pretense, to know His complete forgiveness and unconditional love through humbling conviction and confession. Certainly God is going to lift up the whole church body, men and women, for whom the phrase "spiritual apathy" is an oxymoron, and for whom, when it comes to awakening us as a nation, jealousy and indifference is no obstacle.

An Unwillingness to Believe

The need to understand God by relying on your limited, rational mind can be an obstacle to fully understanding and experiencing the new work of God in our time.

The fear of others' rejection should you voice your need for personal and corporate revival can be an obstacle to knowing God and satisfying the spiritual hunger He's now stirring inside you.

Apathy can erode that very desire for God Himself so much that it fosters a fourth potential obstacle to knowing revival. That obstacle is unbelief.

When you consider the number of people whose lives have been turned inside-out as they have been transformed from an unsatisfying search for meaning to a powerful, personal relationship with God through Jesus Christ—a new life that reaches out to the emotional, spiritual, physical and social needs of others—why would any Christian be unwilling to believe that revival is possible in our time? Why would men and women who truly love God, who are serving Him daily the best they know how, stand at arm's length from revival? What would cause them to say, "I don't believe it's for real. There may be things going on today, unusual, wonderful things of God I can't deny, but I'm just not sure . . . "?

I realize I may have taken the words out of your mouth. When it comes to the possibility of a new spiritual awakening in our country, you may be saying, "I'm not convinced. I don't believe it. I'm not ready to believe it."

In my years of ministry, especially as I've marveled at how the interest and prayer for revival has grown, I've met Christians who are content to stand back and watch.

Something makes them uncomfortable about revival. Their words, body language or mere absence from spiritual gatherings says, "I just don't believe." In my opinion, there are three possible reasons why their unbelief remains an obstacle to their own spiritual awakening.

The first is that some Christians are genuine seekers. God has given them inquisitive hearts that cause them to inspect, analyze and carefully "sift through the evidence" to know the Truth. For them, faith comes through a very involved journey of seeking, listening to and eventually, knowing God. For these people, unbelief is really a reflection of their desire to "know for sure," not a rush to judge, discount or disown something about which they don't care or want to understand.

But there is a second reason Christians are unwilling to believe revival is real in our day. What appears to be unbelief is really an unwillingness to change. Who wants to be disrupted, especially if you're in a comfortable routine of Sunday worship, a youth group your children love and, perhaps, a mid-week Bible study or small group fellowship? Why would you want spiritual awakening, an unpredictable and in some ways disorderly movement of God's Spirit to disrupt a comfortable pattern?

No doubt a baby is more comfortable in the womb and would probably prefer to stay there than make the traumatic journey through the birth canal—even if it means new life.

Are you and I any different? Some today are willing to endure the disruption of their routine that revival would bring. Others are more content to stay where they are and say, "I'm okay. Even though I could be better off, I know it would be too hard, too unsettling, so I'll just go on as I am."

Unbelief in revival can be heard today in a third way, through a much more troubling voice. This is the unbelief of a person feeling convicted of unresolved sin in his or her life. At one time or another throughout the day, this person is you and me. No wonder people, especially Christians who've seen their own sin in the mirror, don't want to look at revival, don't want to admit revival, don't want to believe in revival.

Revival means facing our pride, our selfishness, our greed, our lust, the human rust that has been building up inside of us for years, polluting and hindering the flow of God's Spirit into our lives.

Revival means admitting to God and to others that underneath the make-up and cologne, behind our bluff and boast to make others think we have it all together, we are just like Isaiah who said, "Woe to me, I am ruined." Because revival is all-too real, because the sacrifice of following Christ may seem too costly, those "on the outside looking in" may say, "I don't believe."

Whether we realize it our not, our struggle with the obstacles to revival is not with God but with the adversary who wants to keep us from Him. Without reducing the emerging revival to a struggle between good and evil, one thing is true: without the work of satan in our world, the obstacles that keep you from loving and serving Jesus would not be as big. When God banished satan from His presence, this fallen angel lost what was most precious to him. In a deprived state, he doesn't want anyone to experience what he has now lost. Think of it.

If you were this enemy, you would not want people to know the Word, to know that spiritual awakening can and must come: "Lord, I have heard thy speech and was afraid; O Lord, revive thy work in the midst of the years, in the midst of the years make known; in wrath remember mercy" (Habakkuk 3:2, KJV).

If you were this enemy, you wouldn't want them to know that revival is a return to normal Christianity—a deep, personal, ongoing relationship with Jesus Christ.

If you were this enemy, you would work with individuals and groups—from local churches to parachurch organizations—to bring Christians down to a subhuman level away from the God they had been created to know. How would you do this?

By telling them they don't have time to read the Word.

By telling them all they need is their minds to think through and work out their own problems.

By telling them it isn't necessary to speak up for what they believe.

By telling them things at church are fine, maybe not perfect, but good enough to continue the status quo.

And if you wanted to put up another obstacle between Christians and the God you didn't want them to know, you would tell them that revival is for "other Christians."

The Word says that "As water reflects a face, so a man's heart reflects the man" (Proverbs 27:19). Your focus is what you'll eventually become. If you focus on your weaknesses, your downfalls, your limitations, you'll live life feeling weak, guilty and incomplete. By not being focused in the Word, you won't be focused on God.

Instead, you'll be wandering lost in the darkened cave of this world, unaware that a pinpoint of light, the light of God's Truth, is the only passageway that can lead you back to Christ and a new awakening in Him.

A Question of Attitude

Over the past few years, as I've spoken to churches and parachurch ministries throughout North America, I've seen the above obstacles "come to life" in the form of attitudes in fellow believers. Like me, these are people weighed down with the baggage of original sin, who choose to keep walking, to keep following Christ. Like you and me, they know the obstacles that keep them from being open to spiritual awakening and realizing our one and only true hope in life rests in a personal relationship with Jesus Christ.

The questions I've asked them are the same ones I want to ask you:

How would you describe your need, your desire, your willingness to experience true spiritual awakening?

If God ever brings about another Great Awakening in our land, it will be because He moves in people like you and me who come to Him just as we are. The way you approach the Lord may be inseparably linked to how you approach the need for awakening in your nation and in your life. The way you approach him may be described along a continuum, a "Spectrum of Spiritual Awakening." Where do you find yourself along this spectrum?

*
Antagonistic?

Does this word describe your present attitude? What are the events that have made you antagonistic to God over the past weeks, months and years? Have you ever thought that these feelings are the very things God may use to humble you and bring you to Himself?

*   *
Antagonistic Indifferent?

What does this word feel like to you? Lukewarm? In-between? Is it a word that describes your present relationship with Christ? Billy Graham has suggested that it's possible to be inoculated against the Gospel by receiving just a little bit of it. What is the "little" you've received? What more do you still long to know?

*   *   *
Antagonistic Indifferent Acknowledging?

A word that says "I know something's going on." When you read the Word and see how God has worked in people's lives, you know there's more to life than what you currently have. It's a sigh of relief that says, "I see," and a feeling of anxiousness that says "I want more." Is that what you're acknowledging right now?

*   *   *   *
Antagonistic Indifferent Acknowledging Seeking?

Somewhere, somehow, God broke through your obstacles and you've never been the same. Once you got a taste you had to have more, and so you've followed Him. Which steps of obedience have proved most costly? Which have brought you closest to Him?

*   *   *   *
Antagonistic Indifferent Acknowledging Seeking
*
Involved?

The person who's involved in revival is involved in a life of selflessness. This is a daily habit of loving Jesus because He first loved you (1 John 4:19). Each day you practice this love, a little more of yourself dies and a little more of Jesus begins to live. What would this kind of intimate relationship with Christ look like? What is keeping you from praying for this kind of new awakening in your own life?

Where are you on this continuum? Where is your heart beating in relationship to God who is awakening a nation, one life at a time? Will you be one of those people He uses?

The obstacles to revival are not insurmountable, because the true obstacle to revival is *singular*. It's me. And it's you. God doesn't want any obstacle to spiritual awakening. He just wants you and me to walk with Him every moment of every day. Starting now. As that happens, as the number of footsteps in one, obedient direction increase, we will see revival in our time. We will be tempted to say, "This is what it looks like!"

And the surprise will be on us.

Endnotes

1. Lewis Drummond, telephone conversation, 19 December 1994.

2. Ibid.

3. *Newsweek*, 28 November 1994, 53-62

4. Lewis Drummond, telephone conversation, 4 January 1995.

5. Ibid.

6. Ibid.

7. Joe Aldrich, telephone conversation, 8 February 1994.

8. For a more complete discussion of this material, refer to Charles G. Finney, *Revivals of Religion* (CBN University Press, Virginia Beach, Va., 1978).

9. Dr. Dennis Kinlaw, "A Revival Account Asbury—1970", video © 1988, American Portrait Films, Cleveland, Ohio.

10. Lewis Drummond, telephone conversation, 4 January 1995.

11. Ibid.

CHAPTER SEVEN

What Will the New Awakening Look Like?

As a child growing up on a farm in Mississippi, I was reared on anticipation. I knew the fortunes and security of my family depended on what came down from the sky—steady rain and warm sun to grow our garden, soybeans, cotton and corn that meant food and income. Though I was only a child, I remember how all of life changed every August. Something was happening, something important that demanded the attention of everyone in our family.

The harvest was approaching.

I remember asking questions. I had a deep desire to know exactly when the harvest would be ready. This was something so momentous, so big, I wanted to be part of it.

I asked my uncle, "When is it going to happen, Uncle Millard? When will the harvest come?"

Always his response was, "Wait. Just wait, Tom. I know you're excited. I know the fields look ripe. I can't tell you when it will happen." Then he'd turn his gaze from the green, rolling fields, look into my eyes and say, "When the time comes, you and I will know it. It will be obvious."

Today I am in my mid-forties. Though I no longer live on a farm, the sense of anticipation I felt as a child is still very much a part of who I am. As an adult I'm still curious, still excited about the future. Today the "fields" that preoccupy me are not soybeans and cotton, but a landscape of lives, Christians from all denominations and walks of life. In my brief lifetime I've seen this landscape of the Church in various seasons of growth and seeming stagnation. In the past several years, frankly, a number of men and women in the Church have looked withered. They seem to have lost their vitality. Some seem to have lost their will to grow.

But they are a shrinking majority. Over the past decade something remarkable has been happening in our nation and in the Church. Something has begun to change. I see it when I hear about a pastor named Larry Mancini. A few years ago he was content to serve his congregation in Bayshore, New York. Then Larry met some fellow pastors and church leaders on Long Island—men and women who felt called to pray for their region.

A few years ago, Larry would have spent Tuesday night taking a well-deserved time-out after a busy weekend. Yet on a Tuesday not too long ago he found himself riding with a group of local pastors who were headed to the Brooklyn Tabernacle. They went not for a worship service or a concert featuring a big-name Christian celebrity, but to a prayer meeting. When he came out of the church that evening, Larry said, "I knew God had touched everyone in our group. Through prayer, I knew He was working in me."[1]

What God Asks of Us

Something is happening in our nation. Aware Christians can tell it when a man named Bill McCartney gathers seventy-two men together in 1990 to seek God and when, in four short years, that group mushrooms into stadium-sized and small group gatherings across America with an attendance totaling two hundred eighty thousand. These men have come together to ask the question, "What does it mean to honor Jesus Christ, to become a man of integrity, to become a promise keeper?"

Something is happening to our nation when Henry Blackaby's book, *Experiencing God*, sells thousands of copies because it speaks to people about a quality and depth of relationship with the Lord for which they long.

Something is happening to our nation when International Renewal Ministries receives dozens of requests from pastors and church leaders across the United States and abroad who want to experience the reconciliation, the community, the unity of the Spirit that comes only through humbling confession, deep-felt conviction and repentance.

Something is happening not only in our nation but in Canada as well, when sixty-five thousand Christians gather simultaneously in cities across their country to pray for God to bring revival to their nation.

Something is happening to our nation when more than a quarter of a million teenage youth willingly turn their backs on the temptation to become sexually active and instead pledge to their family, friends—and most of all to God—that they'll wait and preserve that most intimate human relationship for their marriage night.

Something is happening in our nation when a man like Bill Bright, who as founder and president of Campus Crusade for Christ International has experienced many personally significant spiritual milestones, conducts a forty-day fast that he describes as "the greatest spiritual experience of my life."[2] When he tells seven hundred Christian leaders gathered in Orlando, Florida, "We need revival to come," then asks them to pray for two million Americans to fast forty days, I know this is not merely a dream of Bill Bright, it is the definite work of God.[3]

These are the kinds of things that cause me to sit up and take notice that something deeply profound, deeply spiritual is taking place across our country. Something that's bringing new life to a Church that's shown signs of withering. Something that goes to the root of our need for the only One who can truly give us new life. Something that's as inevitable as rain and as necessary as harvest. Something called revival, the revival of Christ's church—you and me—which will be followed by many men and women making first-time commitments to Christ.

Today when I look at the national landscape called the American Church, I sense the childhood anticipation of the harvest building in me once again. I feel it build when I see all that is happening in the lives of broken and renewed pastors, confident teenagers and committed men. I feel a genuine excitement when I see how God is working in their lives and the lives of others with an increasing urgency and intensity that this nation has not seen since the time of Charles Finney and the Great Prayer Revival of 1857. I feel myself leaning forward when I see these people being led to pray and fast and come clean with God in ways they never imagined. I see these and other signs of spiritual awakening in our land and I want to know "When? When, will our country know a full-fledged spiritual awakening? When will it come, Lord? When will we see You fully restore this nation, our nation, to the ways of justice, purity, obedience and faith?"

And though I feel the anticipation, already I know the answer. It was the same one I heard as a farm child looking for an earlier harvest: Wait.

And so while I look forward to the day of revival in the United States, while I chuckle at my own insatiable desire to "know when," I wait. And I pray. My greatest prayer is that God would engulf our nation and all who claim to follow Christ in a sweeping movement of His Spirit. My prayer is that He would revive Christians, starting with me, and that this new breath of His Spirit would awaken new and old believers to a fresh, deepening love for Christ. I know this is the prayer of many believers, men and women who are just as eager as I am for revival to come. I know that whether they admit it or not, they live with their own questions. If you have prayed for revival, if this book has caused you to seek spiritual awakening for the first time, then the same questions may be stirring inside you, too. Questions such as:

How close are we to full-fledged revival?

What will it look like personally and corporately?

Will we know revival when it comes? And if so, how will we know?

What leads us to ask these questions? Is it because we're too impatient, too curious to wait? Do we want to know the exact time, size and shape of revival because as human beings we like certainty more than mystery? Is it because we want the puzzle solved?

I believe the answer to all of the above is yes. I also believe revival is a lot like a long-awaited farm harvest—its timing is out of our hands. As Uncle Millard said, "When the time comes, you and I will know it. We'll know it. It will be obvious."

I happen to agree. The Lord did not ask us to be His timekeepers. He asked us to be His followers, "To act justly and to love mercy and to walk humbly with your God" (Micah 6:8). If in our eagerness we say we "can't wait" for God to revive our land, it's because we long so for Jesus Christ. If spiritual awakening is our prayer, it's only because we pray that strangers and relations may know Him and His salvation, and that we, ourselves, may know His same forgiving, life-giving love *as if for the first time*.

If revival does in fact come in God's own time, what are we to do in the meantime? You and I can pray that we'll be open to receive all that He has to give the Church and our nation when He breathes life back into our hearts, our minds, our very being. As we wait, we can be inspired by the growing evidence of God's unfolding work in our nation. We can revel in stories like the ones you've read. We can look at these glimpses of what He's doing as snapshots—small, focused, yet important glimpses of the "big picture."

Snapshots are wonderful ways to get our attention and stir our curiosity. They're easy to hand to people. They're fun to share. When you pass along these snapshots, stories you've read, you're telling a part of the story of a God who is now stirring His people to love and serve Christ and others. By helping others focus on revival for a minute or a lunch hour, you actually stir yourself and others to ask, "Is this all that God's doing? Is there something more I'm missing? How can I allow Him to flow through me, to use me?"

That "something more" is all the many, individual ways He's moving in people today, stories you and I may never hear. That something more is stories that make up the large panorama of the spiritual awakening that is now dawning across America.

If stories are the snapshots that detail the many instances of *individual* revival now taking place, then principles are the broad brush strokes that create the big picture of corporate, or national, revival. While a snapshot is meant to be held, such a broad panorama can only be viewed by stepping back. And so I'm going to ask you to lay aside the stories you've heard for a moment and step back to see the bigger picture of spiritual awakening.

Let me be clear: what we're going to look at is not a window on the future. The purpose is not to assume that you or I can know what revival will look like; the goal is not to think we can sneak a peak at the Master's painting while His work is still in progress.

The goal is to know the Master Himself!

Most Christians today are unfamiliar with the big picture principles of revival. One reason is because they are unfamiliar with James Burns, a student of revival, whose book, *Revivals, Their Laws and Leaders*, is a forgotten classic. Periodically a work is produced that transcends time. Burns' volume, written in 1909 and last published in 1960, is such a book. In his volume, Burns identifies eleven laws or principles of revival. In no way are they similar to Finney's "Seven Indicators." These principles don't tell us what to look for. Though they're intriguing, though they draw us again and again to Scripture, they aren't clues for coming revival as much as they're foundational truths about how spiritual awakening has taken place throughout history.

- *The Principle of Ebb and Flow*

Communication of any big truth, such as spiritual awakening, rests somewhat on an effective analogy or word picture. In illustrating revival, Burns uses the image of a wave. "Any progress (that moves us closer in our relationship toward God, [sic])," he wrote, "is like the incoming tide. Each wave is a revival, going forward, receding, and being followed by another. To the onlooker it seems as if nothing is gained, but the force behind the ebb and flow is the power of the tide."[4]

Burns understood that the movement of God through revival has come in waves. Like a wave, every major spiritual awakening has built over time as individuals have come together in Christ. Like a wave, when a movement such as the First or Second Great Awakening began to roll, no one could stop it; its momentum, like the wave of the Spirit itself, was the unseen and unstoppable work of God.

In terms of mounting energy and force, Burns' wave analogy is an appropriate one. If you can think of revival as an expression of God's desire to draw close to His creation, you can appreciate Burns' observation that "Revivals are necessary to push humankind to higher planes."[5] In other words, from age to age, God knows we need to be awakened. As much as human nature creates an undertow that drags us down, God responds by moving us forward. As Burns wrote, "Behind the ebb and flow is the unrelenting tide of His redemptive purposes."[6]

Think of how the "wave action" of revival makes sense.

Like a wave, our age will have its own peculiar characteristic. The activity of prayer, the turning to God we see building gradually today, is unique from any other spiritual tide in history.

Like a wave, revival will crest at some point. The culmination will be relatively short before the wave follows its natural course and recedes. It's impossible to live "at the peak" or "on the crest" forever. A revival will move us to new heights and revitalize us. Like reaching the top of a mountain, we know our time on the summit is limited. The time comes to move on. The exhilaration of the view is what inspires us when we go back down to live in the valley. This is the ebb and flow of revival; spiritual awakening itself lasts only briefly, but its impact can linger much longer.

Where have you felt God at work in your own life? In the "ebb" of being drawn back to the truth of your own broken nature? Or in the "flow" of His unseen but very real power moving you forward to Himself? Both movements are from the same loving God. "The Law (or Principle) which moves the mighty tides of the ocean," wrote Burns, "is the same which ruffles the surface of the little pool made by the rain on a summer afternoon."[7]

- *The Principle of Spiritual Growth*

The goal of revival is not to get caught up in guessing when the wave will start. The goal of revival is knowing the Father. The goal is spiritual growth—not just growth of the individual, but growth of the church toward a new level of dedication and spirituality. One of the greatest examples of this was seen in Savonarola, the noted Italian preacher of the Florentine Revival in fifteenth century Italy. As a young man he spent hours at the altar in prayer. Burdened over the world's rejection of Christ and salvation, he fasted, prayed night and day, and poured over Scriptures.

When he was thirty-seven, Savanarola began his most powerful preaching. He was fearless in his cry for repentance. The population of Florence flocked to see and hear him. The crowds pressed each other so close there was barely room to breathe. His words were filled with God's indignation. People wept. They cried to God for mercy. He preached that the Church would be renewed in their time and that before it occurred, God would strike Italy with a fearful chastisement. Savanarola's words heralded the Reformation and proved to be prophetic.

The Principle of Spiritual Growth is that through revival, just as in Savanarola's day, the spiritual and moral temperament of the whole community is changed.

Imagine how your own community—your church, your school, the neighborhood you call home—might be changed by a spiritual awakening. Imagine what spiritual growth could occur.

- *The Principle of Providence/Sovereignty*

Savanarola surely admitted that anything he said or did was part of God's divine plan. And because spiritual awakening occurs on God's timetable, not ours, His Sovereign will always remains in charge. Like the wave action of the ocean, revival is always under His control, and for all its power it is orderly. Even though we know His Providence is at work, we can't determine exactly when the wave will hit. This is consistent with Scripture: "The secret things belong to the Lord our God" (Deuteronomy 29:29). Though we can perceive the indicators of revival—thanks to the human insights of a gifted, godly person such as Charles Finney—the sovereignty of God is the final determining factor in any revival.

Consider the time and energy you might spend on pondering the "what ifs" of revival. What would happen if you invested that same effort in considering the nature and characteristics of God? Might the way you view Him change the way you understand and view revival?

- *The Principle of the Dry Season*

Look at any spiritual awakening in history, including those that have occurred in our country, and you'll discover an obvious, common thread: revival is always preceded by spiritual deadness. It can be the lawlessness in 1800 that preceded the Cane Ridge Awakening or the indifference that defined the mood and times of New York City prior to Jeremiah Lanphier's first noontime prayer meeting in 1857. In the book of Revelation we learn that John was instructed to write the church at Sardis to say "you have a reputation of being alive, but you are dead" (Revelation 3:1).

In the dry season of the Church, there may be outward signs of life, but the people's hearts may have stopped beating. Deadness, despondency, unbelief, lethargy and heaviness are all synonymous with the dry season that always precedes revival. To use the analogy of the wave action, the dry season would be the trough, the tide at its lowest ebb. This does not make the dry season any less a part of revival; God is still sovereign, still in charge. The trough is just as much a part of the wave as the white cap.

Is it possible that the dry season of your church, your community, your nation, may be part of revival? Is it possible that, at some point, we may be coming out of that trough?

- *The Principle of Fullness of Time*

As it continues in all its "fullness," dryness always leads to desperation. Out of their profound sense of dissatisfaction, often with a certain degree of gloom, people begin to cry out to God. We call that prayer. Remember the earlier story of the Hebrides Islands in the late 1940s? A small group of men meeting in a barn began to cry out, "Oh, God, move on your people." Two women, down the road in a neighboring village, began to pray, "Oh, God, move." They cried out because there was nowhere else to turn. Their dryness had led to desperation.

These Christians cried out in prayer in the way most revivals start; they cried out as a remnant. Like other remnants throughout history, these faithful pray-ers languished through a protracted period when their prayers went unanswered. Yet over time, as in other revivals, their numbers gradually increased. Through long, ardent and sacrificial prayers, they laid the foundation for revival. In the Lord's own paradoxical twist, their faithfulness was multiplied.

The story of the Hebrides is the story of virtually every revival: out of a remnant, a large-scale movement is born, a movement that encompasses a large area. And often, strangely enough, the spiritual phenomenon that unfolds is largely unknown! Regardless of how anonymous God's hand is, revival occurs in "the fullness of time." His people in His time live out a principle of patience and faith in which the longings of God's followers are fully expressed.

Has the dry season been allowed to run its course in your life? Imagine the dry season of a nation, in the fullness of time, giving way to desperation. Imagine a remnant in our nation crying out, building momentum, leading a large-scale awakening.

• *The Principle of Leadership*

In any revival, at least one prophet always emerges. Though he or she may be a leader, the person does not "lead" revival in the classic sense of taking control and directing followers to do certain tasks. The prophetic figure in any spiritual awakening doesn't create revival, he or she *interprets* it. The prophet doesn't direct the movement, he or she *embodies* it.

An indelible mark of leadership is the personality of the prophet and the mark he or she makes upon the people. In the Great Shantung Revival of 1927, missionaries were called by the American consulate to the seaport of Chefoo in northern China to wait out the political unrest. While there, they occupied themselves with prayer for healing and for the Chinese people they were committed to serve. One of the leaders of the group, a Norwegian Lutheran woman, scoured the waterfront, aggravating pastors, evangelists and missionaries by asking, "Are you born again?" Her inquisitiveness and personality happened to be the unique contribution that helped stir revival.[8]

Revival is always flavored by the unique personality and mission of the prophet. Against the materialism of his day, St. Francis of Assisi raised the voice of poverty. Out of the Welsh Revival rose the spirited devotion of lay Christians.

Yet despite all leaders' unique personalities, revival is always directed by one person: the Lord Himself. In any spiritual awakening there is always one leader and one leader only—God. Through the Holy Spirit, chosen people embody or epitomize what He is doing for their time.

Think of the most humble, dedicated Christian you know. These qualities of devotion to God, service to others and obedience to the Word, prayer and sacrifice are part of the personality consistent with the people God chooses to embody spiritual awakening.

- *The Principle of Brokenness and Confession*

Brokenness and confession is what the prophet discovers and what the participants in revival experience. When brokenness, confession and repentance begin to occur among God's people, revival spreads with extraordinary swiftness. As every revival in history bears out, individuals and the church as a whole wake up to the seriousness of their own sin. At times, as with the ministers who've attended the Pastors' Prayer Summits, the remorse can be overwhelming. People become very concerned about the open sins of the flesh and the secret sins of the spirit.

As pastors are sensitized to these issues, pointed preaching begins to occur. Usually, however, the greatest brokenness of all occurs in the life of believers as they come to grips with their own lack of love. Normally the result is open and honest confession.

The Principle of Brokenness and Confession yields to a wonderful outcome. As a result of confession and purification of the heart, people become so magnetically attracted to Christ that their dedication grows into a great enthusiasm to follow Him. Naturally, the good news is too life-changing, too wonderful to contain. There's an enthusiasm to serve Jesus and a desire to bring others to Him. The person who experiences this new life in God wants everyone to know the One behind this new reality. This is evangelism in its most contagious form.

When have you ever found yourself so broken, so aware of your sin, that the only thing you could do was come to God and confess? What do you think would happen if the genuine remorse of a few swelled and became the repentance of multiplied thousands in our country? Based on His promise to forgive, how do you suppose the lives of individuals, the life of the church and life as a whole in our nation might change?

• *The Principle of Influence*

A by-product of evangelism supplies one more principle in the natural development of spiritual awakening. As revival progresses—as the wave action builds, as the movement of God crests—large numbers of people discover what only a remnant once knew: Jesus Christ is alive! The influence of revival, however, is not limited merely to a spiritual plane. Awakenings have always spilled over beyond the borders of the Church into the life of their towns and cities.

From the time of Hezekiah to the time of the Wesleys in England, revival's influence is always felt in the political and social structure. One year after revival broke out in Rogue's Harbor, Kentucky (which had been a haven for criminals), the law breakers became the law givers. Previously hardened criminals enthusiastically told others of their new-found faith in Christ. By then many had even become circuit-riding preachers of the Gospel in the American wilderness.

In short, full-fledged revival touches the heart of the whole community. The Church takes on a new role in society; clergy gain new respect. As revived Christians actually live like Christ, they reach out to their schools, work places and neighborhoods in what some would label "social action." Those touched by revival might describe it a little differently. In serving the needs of people out of a renewed heart for God, they know they are really serving Christ.

Can you think of a time when the influence of one person changed an entire group? Think of the greatest social movement of your generation. Then consider that this show of force is only a fraction of the power and influence that could result when God ignites and sustains a movement of His own.

- ## The Principle of Variety

No two spiritual awakenings are exactly alike. While some of their characteristics will be similar, the actual expression of each movement is unique to its own era. In fact, each revival's emphasis is, in many ways, a reaction against the prevailing winds of the day. For instance, Charles Finney's preaching on a Christian's responsibility to conform, confess and receive Christ came in reaction to the hyper-Calvinism that maintained all had been decided beforehand by God, that your salvation or its absence was decided before you were born. The Moravian movement of the eighteenth century was a pendulum swing away from the cold residue of the Reformation.

The variety of spiritual awakening is a testimony to the way God respects and works through the unique strengths of His people and the distinctive climate of each era.

What things are unique about the age in which we live? What is special about the social climate, the problems or sins that trouble you, as a Christian? Can you name some fellow believers who share your views?

- ## The Principle of Recoil

In an unforced, almost natural manner, revival runs its course. Any movement that strikes in one direction creates a reciprocal reaction. If the Church is under a heavy hand of authority, the revival will bring freedom as with the Wesley Revival. If the Church has become so free that it is licentious, the revival will bring authority as it did in the Reformation. The Principle of Recoil then takes effect. As Burns summed it up, "Every revival has a time limit. It has its day, then it recedes."[9] After the wave crests and impacts the shore, the ebb begins. The prophetic "leader" passes on. The Truth endures, the fervor fades.

Through the Principle of Recoil, two things can then happen. The first is that spiritual awakening receives some kind of negative reaction. After the Welsh Revival, a reactionary named J.B. Morgan tried to debunk what God had done by revealing that five years after a hundred thousand had come to Christ, "only" eighty thousand remained. How many pastors, how many laypersons, would love to see a retention rate of 80 percent in their church!

A second characteristic of recoil is that with awakening can also come corruption. The reputation of poverty in the early Franciscan movement, for example, gave way eventually to the people's lust for money. Though no one would equate their ministries with revival, several well-known television evangelists of the 1980s succumbed to money-making schemes to the dismay of disillusioned supporters. Their downfall is the still-recent reminder that the Fall made us sick and that Christ is our only cure.

How large, how significant would revival need to be in this country for the recoil of negativity and corruption to surface? Imagine how powerful, life-changing (and threatening to some) spiritual awakening would be to cause others to rise up in dismay and disbelief, because of personal and national sins.

- *The Principle of Doctrine*

Always, after spiritual awakening runs its God-appointed course, church doctrine moves back to simplicity. This is especially true if the message of the Gospel has been forgotten or overlaid with theology or tradition. Whatever the revival, the message of the Cross has always become central. Every revival, therefore, is a return to God. It's that simple.

Whenever people are moved to know and follow Him, they step up to the reality of their sin and come face-to-face with the only One who can make the necessary sacrifice—Jesus, who overcame death for us on the Cross and through the Resurrection. Revival makes all other issues, all other doctrine, secondary. This is more than a Principle behind a movement. For those who have lived through spiritual awakening, a return to the simplicity of the Cross is the supreme hallmark of returning to the God who "made that which was dead alive again"—through revival.

What is the one doctrine, one Truth in your life that would cause you to pray for revival? When all that is secondary falls away, what is the one, central fact of Christianity upon which your faith, and the hope of this nation, rests?

Where To, Now?

As you consider these Principles of Revival and as you relate them to your own life, with what are you left?

- A sense of expectancy for spiritual awakening in your own lifetime?

- A new conviction of your own brokenness?

- A new awareness of our nation's ungodly ways?

I hope by now you have a much better understanding and deeper appreciation for what revival is, how it develops, how it builds, crests and recedes in God's own time. I hope the wave you're able to picture is more than just a convenient way to think about the last time you enjoyed a warm, sunny beach. I hope Burns' analogy has carried you closer to the real impact revival has made in history and the life-changing force it will one day bring again.

Seen as a whole, these timeless Principles offer more than just the "big picture" of spiritual awakening. As you look at each truth, the real discovery is to see the character of God Himself:

In the *ebb and flow* of revival is God's unseen power to move toward us and work through us in His season and for His reasons.

In the *goal* of revival is God's constant desire for us to grow as His Church.

In the *unknown timetable* of revival is God's providence and sovereignty.

In the *dry season* that precedes revival is God's reminder that without Him we are spiritually dead.

In the *fullness of time* when our dryness leads to desperation, is God's faithfulness to hear our prayers.

In the *"leadership"* of revival are God's purposes and plans embodied in His chosen men and women.

In the *brokenness and confession* of revival is God's life-saving, life-renewing grace of Christ, offered in a way we can best receive it—on our knees.

In the *influence* of revival is God's unique flair for using unique individuals to meet the unique needs of the time.

In the *recoil* of revival is God's infinite ability to work through those who turn their back on Him, even if they claim to be His followers.

In the *doctrine* of revival is God's heart—His Son—whose life, death and resurrection are the heart of every awakening, including the one that awaits us.

When you see God through these Principles, you're seeing revival for what it truly is—a revitalized relationship with Jesus Christ that comes to life in the presence of His reawakened Church, a renewed vessel commissioned to help others know Him. When knowing Him is your personal prayer, revival stops being theoretical and starts becoming deeply personal. When you realize that His Spirit has moved powerfully in history, when you acknowledge He can move again, you can let go of wondering what the next revival will look like or when it will come. When you let the Principles reflect a Person, you will find yourself thinking Him, praising Him, seeking Him, loving Him. That's when you will find yourself waiting on the Lord, praying for His people to be renewed in His time.

Of course, as we find renewed spiritual life, we'll be magnetically drawn to our friends who don't know Christ. We'll naturally introduce them to the greatest Friend of all, thus issuing in what could be the most productive period of evangelism in the history of our world. This result of revival is the ultimate goal of God's own heart and the penultimate reason for revival—the Creator recreating and building His Kingdom here on earth prior to ushering in His eternal Kingdom.

By waiting for revival, I don't mean sitting back and enjoying the view. Waiting means coming to God daily, just as you are. Coming to Him with all your baggage, knowing that He already knows what you're carrying inside. It means coming to Him as one who's been "damaged in shipment." Coming as a broken vessel in need of repair, a vessel that needs to be reshaped because it's the only way to be strong enough to resist the hard knocks that the days ahead are sure to bring.

The call to revival is the call to come home:

To come home from your impossible schedule that has left you out of breath and out of touch with God.

To come home from the trivial diversions that have robbed you of time with the Lord.

To come home from loud radio commercials, loud television shows and other mindless chatter that keeps you from hearing God's still, small voice.

The call to awakening is a call to come to God as a child who has wandered from his or her loving parent. The call to spiritual awakening is to all believers who want to know they are forgiven, accepted and loved again—*for the first time*.

Today a few people in our land have heard this call. They are the ones who have been gripped by conviction, confession and repentance. They are the men and women coming home to the Father they had once forgotten, ignored, or for whom they've simply been too busy. They are like a remnant in a dry season crying,

"Oh God, move. Move in my nation. Move in *me*!"

Is this your voice? Is this your prayer? Do you want to know what it feels like to be alive again? Would you like to come home? Are you already standing on the doorstep?

Endnotes

1. Larry Mancini, telephone conversation, 26 December 1994.

2. National & International Religion Report, 26 December 1994, 1.

3. Ibid.

4. James Burns, *The Laws of Revival* (World Wide Publications, Minneapolis, 1993), 13.

5. Ibid., 14.

6. Ibid., 14.

7. James Burns, *Revivals, Their Laws and Leaders* (Baker, Grand Rapids, Michigan, 1960), 28.

8. Bertha Smith, *Go Home and Tell* (Broadman Press, Nashville, Tennesee), 1965.

9. James Burns, *The Laws of Revival* (Minneapolis: World Wide Publications, 1993), 43.

CHAPTER EIGHT

The Most Important Decision of All

T he harbingers of revival in our day are all around us. The evidence is incontrovertible.

Within three weeks after I returned from Orlando, Florida, where nearly seven hundred Christians leaders had prayed and fasted three days for our nation, I saw a lead article in *National & International Religion Report*. For years I had been praying for revival in our nation. In Orlando, the voice of revival was coming through loud and clear:

- "God is calling the Church to a time of consecrated prayer and fasting," said Thomas Trask,

General Superintendent of the Assemblies of God. This is "the beginning of what has to happen."[1]

- When revival comes, "sinners will race to the Church instead of the Church racing to save sinners," said Nancy DeMoss of the DeMoss Foundation.[2]

- "God is visiting the earth," broadcaster Pat Robertson said.[3]

- David Bryant of Concerts of Prayer International said fasting is not an end in itself, but involves setting aside our "ordinary way of living, because something extraordinary is about to happen."[4]

These are not isolated comments. They are singular convictions rising from a chorus of believers stretching the length and breadth of our country:

- Nel Phillips Bruce, a minister of prayer at Highview Baptist Church in Louisville, Kentucky, has grown up in the church. For most of her seventy-five years, she's been the wife of a Southern Baptist pastor and a spiritual leader in her own right. She is not one to exaggerate, but to speak in calm, passionate words about what she sees going on around her.

  "Today there's a hunger that's being born for prayer, like we have not witnessed before. There's a hunger for experiencing what God can do for us and through us. Everywhere I turn, people have become aware of a fresh encounter with God.

"They're realizing they can do nothing without Him and their dependency on Him has been renewed. They're saying 'I want to understand more about God, I want more of Him.'

"I believe this hunger is the forerunner of a spiritual awakening in our country, and of God calling His people to Himself. Because today, there's something in the air. There's an expectancy of moving from our being spiritually dead to our becoming alive, awakened in Christ. God is taking those who are at a point of death and bringing them to new life. He's moving in this world."[5]

- In early 1994, Gene Warr, an Oklahoma City businessman, was as concerned about America's spiritual state as anyone I know. "When I look at the current moral decay in the United States," he said, "it's obvious that many people no longer recognize or respect the difference between right and wrong. Our families are falling apart. Our government is breaking down. In some places, where people are taking the law into their own hands, there are signs of real anarchy. If there's any inkling of revival taking place in our country, I sure don't see it."[6]

Twelve months is not a long time in the span of history, but a lot can happen in a year's time to change one person's opinion. Gene became the leader who planned the training of twenty-three thousand counselors for Promise Keepers. These leaders were part of the quarter of a million men who attended the ministry's national meetings in

1994. What Gene saw come from these meetings convinced him that something extraordinary had already begun to happen in the spiritual fabric of our country.

"When I attended the Promise Keepers' meeting in Anaheim this summer, I turned to my wife, Irma, and said, 'This is a work of God.' I don't think any man or group of men could have orchestrated the coming together of so many men in so many cities, now coming to God in a new obedience, in such a relatively short span of time—just four years.

"This gathering of men that's continuing to grow and spread is the greatest moving of God anywhere in the world. When I look at Promise Keepers and other movements of the Spirit, I trust we're looking at a national revival, and perhaps a worldwide spiritual awakening."[7]

- Back in the late 1960s, Gene struck up a relationship with a nineteen-year-old named Kelly Green. At the time, the young man was involved in the Mormon church. Yet, through the time he spent with Gene and through his own reading of the Scriptures, Kelly renounced his association with the Mormons and committed his life to serving Jesus Christ. At the time, Gene remembers saying to himself, "If he makes it, he'll be a special trophy of God's grace."

Since the 1980s, Kelly Green has preached as a "harvest evangelist" throughout the country.

"About six our seven times in my ministry," Kelly states, "I've seen what a I call a touch of God, an awakening, or revival. The most recent was in Bossier City (Shreveport), Louisiana in September 1994. I was scheduled to preach at two Sunday morning services. When I walked into the building for the 9:30 A.M. service, there was an extraordinary sense of God's presence. This is a church of two thousand members that had spent eight to ten weeks preparing. What I sensed was more than excitement; there was a heaviness, in a good sense, of God.

"As I was preparing to preach, I realized that the service would be televised by video-taped delay to 39,000 homes. Everything was set up. Everything was planned down to the minute. This can be a little intimidating if God begins to move. The further we got into the service, the more I knew the Lord didn't want me to preach. When the time came for me to preach, I said to the congregation of eighteen hundred, "I know this will be a little uncomfortable, or unorthodox for some of you, but what God's laid on my heart is this: I don't need to preach. He's already been speaking to you. What can I add to the anointing of God? If you're ready to come, I want you to get up out of your seat and come right now."

For the next forty-five minutes, that's exactly what people did. That morning 120 people came to Christ. When it was done, everyone in the church knew God had intervened. After the service, Kelly learned that the pastors, staff and leaders had fasted and prayed, alternately, for forty days. "Because of this," says Kelly, "I had a little understanding of why God did what He did."[8]

In a letter he titled "A Glimpse of True Revival," the church's senior pastor, Dr. Fred Lowery, wrote, "Following forty days of prayer and fasting, God showed up! We had prayed specifically that God would show Himself to us in such a way that everyone would be aware of His presence and power. That happened . . . and people are still talking about it."[9]

- Gene Warr's belief about Promise Keepers that "only God could do this" is the same description others are using for unprecedented movements. "The mighty 'Wind of the Spirit of God' has been blowing across the youth of America and across the world. See You at the Pole is one clear witness of this!" says Henry Blackaby, director of the Office of Prayer and Spiritual Awakening for Southern Baptists. "Only God could have initiated such a heart cry and concert of prayer as we have witnessed. It is only the beginning—the sequel is about to unfold, as God continues to call His people to repentance, prayer, revival and spiritual awakening."[10]

- "Something extraordinary is taking place," says David Bryant. "In my travels I've witnessed an unprecedented grassroots prayer movement that I'm convinced will be the precursor of a sweeping moral and spiritual rebirth in America. It may be the most hopeful sign of our times."[11]

- Steve Hall, a Seattle-based prayer leader working with International Renewal Ministries, believes that "People are finally responding to a hunger God has put in their hearts, a response that's grown out of the desperation of our current moral, economic and political climate. Everything we've tried and worked for has not stemmed the tide of spiritual decline. This is what I'm getting from pastors and laypersons alike, a willingness to bring their brokenness to the Lord, a deep heart-felt cry of 'We just want God.' "[12]

- Paul Chaya, pastor of Olney Baptist Church in Philadelphia, does not hesitate to describe what he sees today in his urban neighborhood. "In the last five years Christians have been getting away from church growth programs; I've heard them say, 'We need to pray for God to revive us, because nothing else will work.' "

  "There is a desperation coming from the people in my church—'God, if you don't do it, nothing is going to happen.' And so they are praying. Prayer meetings at our church used to be very mechanical. Now people weep for souls.

  "There's a feeling that revival has not yet come, but that we're going to continue to pray and praise God for the victories."[13]

- Dr. David McKenna, retired president of Asbury Seminary, has noticed a changing, deepening spiritual climate on college campuses. Since writing *The Coming Great Awakening* in 1990, he has become more convinced than ever that America is ripe for spiritual awakening—and that young people, college-age and under, will play a key role.

  "Wherever I've spoken, whether it's Gordon College, Messiah College, Houghton College, or others, I've met a core group of students who are meeting and praying for revival on their campus."[14]

- For evangelist Bob Cryder, revival in the United States is not a matter of "if," but "when."

  "I honestly believe that the coming outpouring (of the Holy Spirit) is being prepared in some hidden, unknown, small place. It may be in a city that is unknown and overlooked.

  "As with Jeremiah Lanphier and Evan Roberts, God, I believe, will lay hold of one who, though unknown, is mighty with God in prevailing prayer. This person's unseen faithfulness will catch God's hand and bring His anointing. How deeply I praise God for the large gatherings around revival in our day, but I believe spiritual awakening will come from the 'small and unknown'—that way God will get all the glory."

An increasing spiritual hunger. A desperation for God. A turning to prayer among our nation's youth, among Christians of all ages. The expectancy and certainty that God is at work in ways we're yet unable to see. A new awareness of revival among people who believed, even months ago, that spiritual awakening was nowhere to be seen on the American landscape.

If spiritual awakening is a thunderous roar of the Spirit, then these are revival's whispers. They may not be audible where you worship or live, but they are real. And by all indications, these heart-cries for God are growing.

Even during the writing of this book, the evidence for revival in our nation continues to mount. There will be more stories, more accounts, more examples of broken, changed lives, all of which will have one explanation: "Only an extraordinary work of the Holy Spirit could bring this about."

And as these occurrences take place, as movements like Promise Keepers spread, as Christians continue to fast and pray, it will be natural to ask yourself, "What do I believe about spiritual awakening in me and in my nation?" As you explore this question, I suspect you'll find yourself in one of three "places" regarding revival:

You may be one who's already experienced a personal revival. Your life may have ebbed until you could do nothing more than come to God out of desperation as your last and only hope. For you, revival is real because you've rediscovered that God is real and alive. No wonder you're praying for awakening to come to your nation, your church, your friends. You've been brought back to life!

In reading this book, you may still feel like someone "on the outside looking in." Spiritual awakening has not been part of your spiritual journey with God. Though you can't deny the power of God in the people and groups you've met in these pages, though you share the same Lord, though you pray and seek to follow His call, revival is still "out there." You're not sure whether spiritual awakening will ever be real in your life—though you're not closing the door, either.

Or, perhaps you find yourself one of the curious. For you, spiritual awakening is neither immediately real, nor is it something you choose to discount or ignore. You're open to whatever God might show you. Praying for revival, talking to others, searching the Scriptures to see how God has awakened others, are not out of the question. In fact, already you find yourself moving in that direction.

Regardless of where you find yourself concerning spiritual awakening, you can prepare yourself for revival. And as you do, you may discover you're part of a global phenomenon that could have its birth right here in this country. Let me leave you with a concluding story.

The Strategic Continent

In 1984 I felt as if I were standing at a crossroads in my life. As a Crusade Director and Director of Counseling and Follow-Up Administration for Mr. Graham, I had been working in Australia and had come to Bristol, England, for the first evangelistic meeting of six Billy Graham crusades called "Mission England." Something had been stirring in me for weeks, a desire to work overseas in evangelism. I went to Walter

Smyth, the Director of International Crusades, and told him about my interest. Though my words surprised him, he was open to my request. My boss at the time, Charlie Riggs, said assuringly, "If God wants you to work overseas, that's fine with me."

When I woke up the next morning, I felt a sense of total gloom. In asking to shift my ministry area from Counseling and Follow-Up to International Ministries, I knew I had done the wrong thing, but I didn't know why. That morning I went back to Walter Smyth, feeling very chagrined. "Please, erase my request from your mind," I said.

I knew I was called to keep working in North America. I knew there was something inside me, something of God, that drew me to serve people beyond my own continent. These two assurances lived within me. Sometimes I agonized about it. Often I prayed, "Lord, you know I desire to see people come to you. You've given me a heart for revival; You've given a heart for Yourself. Then why am I so unsettled?"

Charlie Riggs, my spiritual mentor, colleague and close friend, knew my heart. Out of love, he began to give me overseas assignments. Out of one of these "foreign duties" I experienced a watershed moment of understanding, not only for what God was doing in my life, but for what He's doing today to bring revival to our nation and our world.

The breakthrough came in April 1986. I was busily preparing program materials for "Amsterdam '86," a rare gathering of ten thousand itinerant evangelists from around the world. I found myself hop-scotching across Latin America, North America and Asia to arrange the translation, writing and publication of ministry guides. In between phone calls and ticket windows I continued to pray, "Lord, you know my heart for revival. What does this work, this particular time in my life, have to do with fulfilling the desire You've given me?"

Riding in a cab through a noisy, congested section of Seoul, South Korea, I received my answer. Though I don't pretend to quote God, His voice at that particular moment was crystal clear:

Do Koreans live in North America?

"Yes," I said.

Do Latin Americans live in North America?

"Yes," I said.

Do Europeans live in North America?

Again, I said, "Yes."

For several city blocks, it was as if God read me a roll-call of nations. He brought to mind nearly every continent or country I had ever visited, or knew existed. That afternoon my understanding of my own continent, my own country, changed. Though I was well aware that the United States had become the melting pot for the world's races, that afternoon geography and ministry converged in my heart like a grand "Aha!" *Virtually every race, every people, every ethnic group, could be found in North America. And when revival comes to North America, people from all lands will carry the movement of God to their own people groups.*

I filed this realization away under "God's Calling." From month to month over the next eight years I took it off the shelf, opened my heart to God and asked Him, "What does this mean? I believe you've made North America a strategic part of your plan to bring others to yourself—but how? And what, if anything at all, are you calling me to do?"

In the spring of 1994 I learned the answer. The time had come for me to leave the Billy Graham Evangelistic Association. After twenty years I had been able to invest myself in some very able partners in ministry. One was Rick Marshall whom God had "awakened" at the Pastors' Prayer Summit at Cannon Beach, Oregon.

Out of three possible options, one rose to the top, a ministry I had been aware of for years: International Students, Incorporated (ISI). After ten weeks of prayer and interviews, I accepted the board's offer to become ISI's new president. Their mission rang true:

> ISI exists to share Christ's love with international students, and to equip them for effective service in cooperation with the local church and others.

After just a few weeks on the job, I came face-to-face with these words and their meaning for revival today. I met Abel, a student from southeastern China who was completing a Ph.D. in computer science. He had married an American woman. Both were vivacious Christians and Bible teachers as a part of ISI's ministry at a midwestern university. Abel's coming to America, and the courageous steps he and his wife soon plan to take, are a mini-glimpse at our world's current revival stirrings.

When Abel came to the United States six years ago, he had been a Communist. For six lonely months he had sought friends and found none. Through the love of an International Student Friendship Partner, Abel learned about Jesus Christ, and after several years of searching and study he gave his life to the Lord. He married and determined not to return to China. But as he continued to study God's Word, his own spiritual life deepened. The hope and power of the Gospel was too great to ignore—or to keep to himself. Abel decided he had to return to his homeland. He wanted his people to discover, to meet and to love the Jesus he had come to know.

When Abel and his wife arrive in China they will encounter resistance, rejection and possible persecution from their families and friends. To those who have never heard the name "Jesus" or never seen a Bible, the message of salvation could be an affront—as well as the only answer to every person's search for meaning, purpose and direction in life *if they respond positively to Christ as Lord and Savior*. Some will be able to know life in all its abundance because they'll see Christ alive in Abel and his wife. They will know eternal life because these two people, awakened by the Holy Spirit, are eager to reproduce themselves spiritually.

Abel and his wife are not alone. Suresh is a young man from India also serving with ISI. His life's desire is to help international students now in the United States go back to their respective homes and carry the same

Jesus he's met to their own people.

And there is Connie (not her real name) from South Africa. As one of her country's educational leaders, she came to the United States to get her master's degree in education. She came as a nominal Christian but through vibrant believers in an international setting, her spirit, her meaning for living, was revived. Now she's going back to South Africa not only to help her people become more educated, but to help her people know Christ in a vital, real way.

There's a reason why Abel, Suresh and Connie have come to our continent, our country. *Today the world has come to North America.* The thousands of men and women from nations around the globe who are studying in America's colleges and universities—studying to become leaders in industry, science, education and politics, eager and talented men and women—are open to explore and embrace the Gospel of Jesus Christ.

It's clear to me that God has brought people like Abel, Suresh and Connie to North America for a reason. As the next Great Awakening takes place in North America—as God's work in areas of conviction, confession and repentance eventually builds and crests in a wave of revival—it will be obvious to all who are awakened by God, *including internationals and international students!* In turn, they will be vessels through whom God will spread the Truth of His Son to their respective peoples.

These are the individuals who are meeting Christ today and who will take Him back home to their respective nations, not necessarily as pastors, but as influential leaders in business, politics, education, science and industry. If there is another Great Awakening in America, (and I believe the question is not "If?" but "When?"), I believe the whole world will know it. By awakening the Church in North America, God will be awakening the entire world through women and men who will go back to their homelands with a new Message of vital spiritual life and salvation.

The current revival stirrings on our continent and in our nation do not rest with a ministry like International Students Incorporated, a visionary such as Joe Aldrich, or a layperson such as Gene Warr. Spiritual awakening rests with God alone. Like the tide whose ebb and flow is beyond our control, the Lord who created oceans and who changes lives will revive our nation—in His own time. God's sovereignty is for certain. And so is something else.

"I'm preaching to people who are hungry for more than what just takes place in the average church on Sunday morning," says evangelist Kelly Green. "It's not that they're discontent with their pastor or they don't like their church. Yet there is a definite heart hunger in America for more of God. If God decides to move again, there's going to be a real receptiveness, especially within the forty-and-under crowd who've never seen a move of God, not even to the magnitude of the Jesus movement in the early 1970s."[15]

How Do You Start a Revival?

The hunger for God in our country is only going to grow stronger. In a *Newsweek* magazine cover story, "The Search for the Sacred: America's Quest for

Spiritual Meaning," Charles Nuckolls, an anthropologist at Emory University, notes how "We've stripped away what our ancestors saw as essential—the importance of religion and family. . . ." He's referring to Americans in general, but he might as well have been talking about Christians hungry for a God they once knew when he says, "People feel they want something they've lost, and they don't remember what it is they've lost. But it has left a gaping hole."

"That, in essence," the article concludes, "is the seeker's quest: to fill the hole with a new source of meaning. Why are we here? What is the purpose of our existence? The answers change in each generation, but the questions are eternal."[16]

We in the Church believe that a personal relationship with God through Jesus Christ is the only true answer that can satisfy these eternal questions. If we expect Him to revive our spirits, if we expect God to stir us to new life, then we must be willing to let Him begin the process of personal revival where He must—with all that is dead inside *us*. And that will not be easy.

In her closing address to "A Special Call to Prayer & Fasting for Our Country" in Orlando, Nancy Leigh DeMoss invited everyone in attendance to take a good, hard look past the facade of today's Church to the spiritual interior of our very being, where true personal and national revival starts:

Is it possible that Jesus has lost His place in the Church? On the face of things it would not seem so. We still have prayers and preaching. We still have crosses on our church buildings. Yet, I'm reminded of the Old Testament passage in which God took His Prophet Ezekiel on a tour of the temple. In a vision God showed His servant a hole in the wall of that temple and said, "Ezekiel, look inside the hole and see what is really going on inside." What Ezekiel saw behind the facade of spirituality was unspeakable filth, idolatry and immorality right in the temple of God. The glory of God had departed from the Holy of Holies, and yet God's people, assured by their leaders that everything was fine, continued right on with their religious routines, programs and practices, totally oblivious to the fact that they had lost the manifest presence of God in their midst (Ezekiel 8). . . .

I wonder, if we could get honest enough to let God tear a hole in the wall of our modern-day, respectable Christianity. Could we be honest enough to let Him tear a hole in the wall of our ministries and, even more personally, in the wall of our own hearts so we could see what's really inside? . . .

Oh, for the presence and the power of God! You see, revival is just that sovereign act of God that restores the Lord Jesus to His rightful place as the Lord and the lover of His people. And when the glory of God fills His temple once again, then we will experience what Paul wrote about in 1 Corinthians 14, when lost people will come into our midst and the secrets of their hearts will be laid bare and they will fall on their faces and worship

God and say "Truly, God is in your midst."

Revival is not just another emphasis to add to our already overcrowded agendas. It's not an option. It's not just a nice idea. A meeting with God in genuine revival is our only hope. We know that revival is a sovereign work of God, that it can not be manufactured, that the wind blows as the Spirit directs, that He moves in His way and in His time. But I believe, as someone once said, "Set our sails to catch the winds from heaven— when God chooses to blow upon His people."[17]

One of James Burns' revival Principles, the "Principle of Doctrine," reminds us that God's sovereign, spiritual awakening will take us to the centrality and simplicity of the Cross. All that we can't understand about how or when God will revive our nation and revive us as individuals, hangs on a tree at Calvary, with a dying man brought to life again in three days.

In the resurrected Christ, the new, spiritual awakening which our nation, church, you and I so desperately need has already begun.

"How do you start a revival?" someone once asked the British evangelist, Gipsy Smith. He replied, "If you want to start a revival, go home and get a piece of chalk. Go into your closet and draw a circle on the floor. Kneel down in the middle of the circle and ask God to start a revival inside the chalk mark. When He has answered your prayer, the revival has begun."[18]

Most people think that God can start a revival anytime He wishes. Can He? Will He? The Bible defines active sin thus, "Anyone, then, who knows the good he ought to do and doesn't do it, sins" (James 4:17). If God could start a revival anytime He wanted (as if we were robots), and He *isn't* doing it, or if He's holding back revival from a nation, then He would be guilty of omission by His own principles!

Revival has broken out throughout our nation whenever people have turned themselves to God in godly repentance and humility, weeping over and asking forgiveness for their sins and their selfish lives. This is spiritual awakening—to be a true follower of Christ living in a continual state of revival as a clean vessel for His service. To get a grasp of God in Spirit and in Truth, and then live it, is to know revival—to know *Christ*—for yourself.

This is the most important decision of all: will you choose to seek Him, to love Him and to follow Him? Are you open to the new awakening God wants to bring about *in you*?

Endnotes

1. *National & International Religion Report*, 26 December 1994, 1.

2. Ibid.

3. Ibid.

4. Ibid.

5. Nel Phillips Bruce, telephone conversation, 20 January 1995.

6. Gene Warr, telephone conversation, 25 January 1994.

7. Gene Warr, telephone conversation, 10 January 1995.

8. Kelly Green, telephone conversation, 10 January 1995.

9. Fred Lowery, letter to Kelly Green, 2 October, 1994.

10. Henry Blackaby, letter to National Network for Youth Ministries, 6 January 1993.

11. David Bryant, address at "Something's Happening USA" conference, San Diego, 30 December, 1993.

12. Steve Hall, telephone conversation, 7 December 1994.

11. Paul Chaya, telephone conversation, 5 January 1995.

14. David McKenna, telephone conversation, 10 January 1995.

15. Kelly Green, telephone conversation, 10 January 1995.

16. Barbara Kantrowitz, "In Search of the Sacred," *Newsweek*, 28 November 1994, 55.

17. Nancy Leigh DeMoss, address to "A Special Call to Prayer & Fasting for Our Country", Orlando, Florida, 7 December 1994.

18. Bob Norsworthy, on-line computer correspondence, 1 November 1994.

Preparing for Personal Revival

Neither you nor I can create revival—but we can prepare for it. Like Hezekiah who sought the Lord, you can come to God just as you are, with everything that concerns you, saddens you and moves you about the condition of our nation today. You can prepare yourself for your own personal revival by asking yourself some very basic questions that follow, as noted in *Spirit of Revival* magazine, March 1995, pp. 37-39. Treat them as a kind of "personal inventory of the heart," *your* heart. How do you feel toward God and all that He can and will do through you in the coming days?

Before you look at these questions, take to heart these simple suggestions:

Pray the prayer of the psalmist: "Search me, O God, and know my heart; test me and know my anxious thoughts. See if there is any offensive way in me, and lead me in the way everlasting" (Psalm 139: 23,24).

Be totally honest as you answer each question.

Agree with God about each need He reveals in your life. Confess each sin, with the willingness to make it right and forsake it.

Praise God for His cleansing and forgiveness.

Renew your mind and rebuild your life through meditation and practical application of the Word of God.

Review these questions periodically to remain sensitive to your need for ongoing revival.

I've grouped the questions in key categories to help focus their impact:

Genuine Salvation

Therefore, if anyone is in Christ, he is a new creation; the old has gone, the new has come! (2 Corinthians 5:17).

1. Was there ever a time in my life that I genuinely repented of my sin?

2. Was there ever a time in my life that I placed my trust in Jesus Christ alone to save me?

3. Was there ever a time in my life that I completely surrendered to Jesus Christ as the Master and Lord of my life?

God's Word

Oh, how I love your law! I meditate on it all day long . . . Your promises have been thoroughly tested, and your servant loves them (Psalm 119:97,140).

1. Do I love to read and meditate on the Word of God?

2. Are my personal devotions consistent and meaningful?

3. Do I practically apply God's Word to my everyday life?

Humility

For this is what the high and lofty One says—he who lives forever, whose name is holy: "I live in a high and holy place, but also with him who is contrite and lowly in spirit, to revive the spirit of the lowly and to revive the heart of the contrite (Isaiah 57:15).

1. Am I quick to recognize and agree with God in confession when I have sinned?

2. Am I quick to admit to others when I am wrong?

3. Do I rejoice when others are praised and recognized but my accomplishments go unnoticed by others?

4. Do I esteem all others as better than myself?

Obedience

Obey your leaders and submit to their authority. They keep watch over you as men who must give an account. Obey them so that their work will be a joy, not a burden, for that would be of no advantage to you (Hebrews 13:17).

1. Do I consistently obey what I know God wants me to do?

2. Do I consistently obey the human authorities God has placed over my life (those who do not contradict God's moral law)?

Pure Heart

If we confess our sins, he is faithful to forgive us our sins and purify us from all unrighteousness (I John 1:9).

1. Do I confess my sins specifically?

2. Do I keep "short sin accounts" with God (confess and forsake as He convicts)?

3. Am I willing to give up all sin for God?

Clear Conscience

So I strive always to keep my conscience clear before God and man (Acts 24:16).

1. Do I consistently seek forgiveness from those I wrong or offend?

2. Is my conscience clear with every person? (Can I honestly say, "There is no one I have ever wronged or offended in any way and not gone back to them and sought their forgiveness and made it right"?)

Priorities

But seek first his kingdom and his righteousness and all these things will be given to you as well (Matthew 6:33).

1. Does my schedule reveal that God is first in my life?

2. Does my checkbook reveal that God is first in my life?

3. Next to my relationship with God, is my relationship with my family my highest priority?

Values

Therefore, as God's chosen people, holy and dearly loved, clothe yourself with compassion, kindness, humility, gentleness and patience (Colossians 3:12).

1. Do I love what God loves and hate what God hates?

2. Do I value highly the things that please God (e.g., giving, witnessing to those without Christ, studying His Word, prayer, helping and serving others)?

3. Are my affections and goals fixed on others and eternal values?

Sacrifice

But whatever was to my profit I now consider loss for the sake of Christ (Philippians 3:7).

1. Am I willing to sacrifice whatever is necessary to see God move in my life and church (time, convenience, comfort, reputation, pleasure, etc.)?

2. Is my life characterized by genuine sacrifice for the cause of Christ, for righteousness and justice?

Spirit Control

But the fruit of the Spirit is love, joy, peace, patience, kindness, goodness, faithfulness, gentleness and self-control. Against such things there is no law. Those who belong to Christ Jesus have crucified the sinful nature with its passions and desires. Since we live by the Spirit, let us keep in step with the Spirit. Let us not become conceited, provoking and envying each another (Galatians 5:22-26).

1. Am I allowing Jesus to be Lord of every area of my life?

2. Am I allowing the Holy Spirit to "fill" my life each day?

3. Is there consistent evidence of the fruit of the Spirit being produced in my life?

First Love

For to me, to live is Christ and to die is gain . . . . I am torn between the two: I desire to depart and be with Christ, which is better by far (Philippians 1:21,23).

1. Am I as much in love with Jesus as I have ever been?

2. Am I thrilled with Jesus, filled with His joy and peace, and making Him the continual object of my love?

Motives

Peter and the other apostles replied: "We must obey God rather than men!" (Acts 5:29).

1. Am I more concerned about what God thinks about my life than about what others think?

2. Would I pray, read my Bible, give and serve as much if nobody but God ever noticed?

3. Am I more concerned about pleasing God than I am about being accepted and appreciated by others?

Moral Purity

But among you there must not be even a hint of sexual immorality, or of any kind of impurity, or of greed, because these are improper for God's holy people. Nor should there be obscenity, foolish talk or coarse joking, which are out of place, but rather thanksgiving (Ephesians 5:3-4).

1. Do I keep my mind free from books, magazines, or entertainment that could stimulate ungodly fantasizing or thoughts that are not morally pure?

2. Are my conversation and behavior pure and above reproach?

Forgiveness

Therefore, as God's chosen people, holy and dearly loved, clothe yourselves with compassion, kindness, humility, gentleness and patience. Bear with each other and forgive whatever grievances you may have against one another. Forgive as the Lord forgave you (Colossians 3:12-13).

1. Do I seek to resolve conflicts in relationships as soon as possible?

2. Am I quick to forgive those who wrong me or hurt me?

Sensitivity

Therefore, if you are offering your gift at the altar and there remember that your brother has something against you, leave your gift there in front of the altar. First go and be reconciled to your brother; then come and offer your gift (Matthew 5:23-24).

1. Am I sensitive to the conviction and promptings of God's Spirit?

2. Am I quick to respond in humility and obedience to the conviction and promptings of God's Spirit?

Evangelism

He told them, "This is what is written: The Christ
will suffer and rise from the dead on the third day.
. . . You are witnesses of these things" (Luke
24:46-48).

1. Do I have a burden for those who don't know
Christ?

2. Do I consistently witness for Christ?

Prayer

I urge, then, first of all, that requests, prayers,
intercession and thanksgiving be made for everyone (1 Timothy 2:1).

1. Am I faithful in praying for the needs of others?

2. Do I pray specifically, fervently and faithfully for
revival in my life, my church and our nation?

REMEMBER

YOU, IF NO ONE ELSE,
CAN BE A WALKING REVIVAL!

Resource Guide

The following organizations and individuals mentioned in *Revival Signs: The Coming Spiritual Awakening* would be pleased to send you more information about their respective ministries in spiritual awakening, evangelism and prayer.

Baptist Home Mission Board
Henry Blackaby
Director of Prayer for Spiritual Awakening
1350 Spring Street Northwest
Atlanta, GA 30367

Phone: (404) 898-7000
Fax: (404) 898-7340

Baptist Sunday School Board (True Love Waits)

Sponsored by the Baptist Sunday School Board, True Love Waits is an international campaign designed to challenge teenagers and college students to remain sexually pure until marriage.

The Baptist Sunday School Board
An Agency of the Southern Baptist Convention
127 Ninth Ave. N., Nashville, TN 37234

Phone: 1-800-588-9248
Fax: (615) 251-5055

Bayshore Church of the Nazarene
Larry Mancini, Pastor
Montauk Drive and Pine Acres Boulevard
Bay Shore, New York 11706

Phone: (516) 666-6676
Fax: (516) 666-6689

Billy Graham Evangelistic Association
1300 Harmon Place
Minneapolis, MN 55403

Phone: (612) 338-0500
Fax: (612) 335-1318

Bruce, Nel
P.O. Box 91363
Louisville, KY 40291

Phone: (502) 239-1888, 239-3353

Campus Crusade for Christ, International
100 Sunport Lane
Orlando, FL 32809

Phone: (407) 826-2100
Fax: (407) 826-2120

Concerts of Prayer International

Centered on the Lord Jesus Christ, the mission of Concerts of Prayer International is to serve the Church by promoting, equipping, and mobilizing movements of united prayer that seek God for spiritual awakening and worldwide evangelization.

P.O. Box 1399
Wheaton, IL 61089

Phone: (708) 690-8441
Fax: (708) 690-0160

Cryder, Bob; Team Ministries

Mission Statement: Bob Cryder Team Ministries is dedicated to calling the Church back to her Head, the Lord Jesus Christ (revival), equipping her to follow Him (discipleship) and with her, pressing to present the Good News of Jesus Christ to this lost generation (evangelism).

P.O. Box 14845
Portland, OR 97214-0845

Phone: (503) 238-4728
Fax: (503) 238-3905

Green, Kelly; Evangelistic Association

As a harvest evangelist who communicates the Gospel in a timely, relevant manner, Kelly Green speaks to local churches throughout the U.S., with a special emphasis on students.

P.O. Box 6749
Mobile, AL 36660

Phone: (334) 660-8502
Fax: (334) 660-8262

International Renewal Ministries
(Pastors' Prayer Summits)

A Prayer Summit is a prolonged, four-day, life-changing worship experience attended by a diversity of Christian leaders from specific, targeted communities whose singular purpose is to seek God, His Kingdom, and His righteousness with the expectation that He will create and guide them through a humbling, healing, uniting process which will lead them to a unity of heart, mind and mission and will qualify them for the blessing of God.

8435 N.E. Glisan St.
Portland, OR 97220

Phone: (503) 251-6455
Fax: (503) 254-1268

International Students Incorporated

International Students, Inc., exists to share Christ's love with international students and to equip them for effective service in cooperation with the local church and others.

P.O. Box "C"
Colorado Springs, CO 80901

Phone: (719) 576-2700
Fax: (719) 576-5363

Life Action Ministries

Mission Statement: "To give birth to and/or nurture revival among God's people resulting in a Spiritual Awakening among the lost."

2000 Morris Drive
Niles, Michigan 49120
Phone: (616) 684-5905
Fax: (616) 684-0923

National Network for Youth Ministries
(See You at the Pole)

Mission Statement: "To link youth workers for encouragement and spiritual growth, and to share recourses for more effective ministry. As a result, every teenager can be exposed to the Gospel, discipled toward a biblical lifestyle, established in a local church and equipped to help reach the world."

17150 Via del Campo
Suite 102
San Diego, CA 92127

Phone: (619) 451-1111
Fax: (619) 451-6900

New Discovery Community Church
Richard L. Twiss, Presiding Elder
3504 N.E. 49th Street
Vancouver, WA 98661

Phone: (360) 695-2234
Fax: (360) 694-2901

Olney Baptist Church
Paul Chaya, Pastor
239 West Chew Avenue
Philadelphia, PA 19120

Phone: (215) 548-8833

Promise Keepers
Promise Keepers is a Christ-centered ministry dedicated to uniting men through vital relationships to become godly influences in their world.

P.O. Box 18376
Boulder, CO 80308

Phone: (303) 421-2800

Tharp, James W.
School of Prayer
5595 Love Lane
Bozeman, MT 59715

Phone: (406) 586-7760